SURVIVING
DEPRESSION

SURVIVING
DEPRESSION

A Catholic Approach

SECOND EDITION

Kathryn J. Hermes, FSP

auline
BOOKS & MEDIA
Boston

Library of Congress Cataloging-in-Publication Data

Hermes, Kathryn.
  Surviving depression : a Catholic approach / Kathryn J. Hermes. -- Updated
and expanded ed.
    p. cm.
  Includes bibliographical references.
  ISBN-13: 978-0-8198-7225-8
  ISBN-10: 0-8198-7225-3
  1. Depressed persons--Religious life. 2. Depression, Mental--Religious
aspects--Catholic Church. I. Title.
  BV4910.34.H47 2012
  248.8'625--dc23
                              2012006156

Cover design by Rosana Usselmann

Published by Pauline Books & Media, 50 Saint Pauls Avenue, Boston, MA 02130-3491

Printed in the U.S.A.

www.pauline.org

Pauline Books & Media is the publishing house of the Daughters of Saint Paul, an international congregation of women religious serving the Church with the communications media.

3 4 5 6 7 8 9   21 20 19 18 17

*Dedicated to those everywhere
who have the courage to walk in the darkness
toward the light*

Contents

CHAPTER 11

Healings Are Not "Success Stories"

≋ 141 ≋

Conclusion:
Eight Steps to Inner Peace

≋ 147 ≋

Epilogue

≋ 171 ≋

Notes

≋ 175 ≋

Introduction

Depression Has Many Faces

If you have picked up this book, you are most likely wondering if "surviving" depression is possible for you or someone you know. Perhaps you are grasping at one more glimmer of hope that your or another's depression might be lifted. It is estimated that one in ten Americans today meet the criteria for recurring depression. Almost half of these meet the criteria for major depression.[1] Major depression is the number one psychological disorder in the western world.[2] At the rate of increase of instances of depression that we are seeing today, particularly among the young, by 2020 depression will be the second most debilitating disease in the western world.[3] In recent years there has been a surge of information about depression in the clinical and popular arena. Talking about depression and its effects on people's lives has become acceptable even in public programming on radio talk shows and television interviews, internet sites, blogs, Facebook pages, etc. However, the essential link between surviving this illness and faith is still an area that cries out to be explored. I have received many letters and phone calls from people who have read the first edition of *Surviving Depression: A Catholic Approach* confirming that it was precisely this link between what they were experiencing and faith that was the most helpful. The book has been translated into at least ten languages, indicating that depression, unfortunately, is a widespread problem.

New causes of concern have arisen in the past ten years or so. People have had to find within themselves strength in the face of terrorism and vigilance before the constant threat of a new attack on our country. The sex abuse crisis in the Catholic Church, and the disillusionment in the Church's leaders that accompanied it, has been deeply disturbing. Katrina, as well as other hurricanes, tornadoes, floods, fires, earthquakes, and other natural disasters have forced people from their homes and destroyed their livelihoods. Our country is again at war, and some of us are keenly aware of the effect that war has had on our families and on ourselves. Daily we face overwhelming amounts of information and impossible demands on our attention and time. Some of us bear the added burden of a mental illness, psychological vulnerability, the effects of abuse, or depression that is a consequence of a situation we cannot control, the side-effect of medication, or of another illness. From the perspective of faith and the resources that are available to us through spirituality, this book addresses those who are suffering from depressive illness, disillusionment, dark moods, and emotional vulnerability.

I am not a psychologist. I am not a theologian. My claim to credibility in writing *Surviving Depression: A Catholic Approach* is that I have been seriously depressed and have spent a lot of time struggling with God through the years I lived with depression. I know depression from the inside. I know the spiritual anguish it brings. I know the loneliness, the isolation, the fear of "losing it," and I believe one truly understands depression not by studying or reading about it, but by living with it.

In June of 1985, I was admitted to Saint Elizabeth's Hospital in Brighton, Massachusetts for simple outpatient surgery. I went into the surgery a healthy, strong, ambitious, and articulate young woman of twenty-one. I came out of the recovery unit with something terribly wrong. Four days later, I was told that I had had a stroke. I was paralyzed on my right side. I couldn't stand up. I had no strength. I had lost much of my memory. I couldn't use even the most basic vocabulary. Two weeks and many tests later, I was released from the hospital and began an eighteen-year journey of rehabilitation.

Though I recovered much of my strength and coordination within the first few years, for the following twelve years I seemed unable to regain my emotional stability. I quickly found myself in a manic-depressive cycle that became increasingly more pronounced. Violent mood swings sent me crashing between effervescent periods of incredible activity and black nights of paralyzing depression. Twelve years after my stroke I would be diagnosed with Temporal Lobe Epilepsy (TLE), a bipolar organic disorder—which brought about another cycle of depression as I began to live with a new "label."

God Has Many Faces

During those first weeks after the stroke, I clearly remember thinking: *God has given me this stroke and I will accept it with graciousness. This is the will of God and God certainly has some reason for it.* And I accepted it with peace . . . or so I thought. It took six years for me to realize how angry I was—angry at God, angry at everyone around me, angry at the world. At that time, I began regular spiritual direction. The more I shared of what was in my heart, the angrier I became, and the farther away God seemed. I could not understand what possible meaning this cross could have. I spent a year unable to believe God even existed. In this spiritual "blackout," I read over and over again the second part of the book of Isaiah, though the words were like sandpaper to my heart:

> O afflicted one, storm-tossed, and not comforted,
>> I am about to set your stones in antimony,
>> and lay your foundations with sapphires.
> I will make your pinnacles of rubies,
>> your gates of jewels,
>> and your wall of precious stones (54:11–12).

As the cycle of depressions came and went, with confusion and despair clouding my vision, I wrestled with God, trying to understand just one question: *Why me?* Though I never received an answer to that question, was never given a clue to understanding the meaning of my suffering, I was gradually—very gradually—able to realize that it was no longer an issue for me. I didn't need an answer; I could live with the mystery.

Depression spares no one. Christians become as depressed as anyone else does; priests and men and women religious suffer from depression. Teens in the flower of youthful dreams become depressed. Even children can become depressed. It might seem that people who have faith or a future should have no reason to be depressed. They should be able to pray, dream, or will themselves out of it. It is hard to reconcile depression— what many still incorrectly see as a moral deficiency—with faith in the power of God. However, depression is just an expression of our fragile human vulnerability. Ironically, this empty darkness is often the source of immense creativity, the black night that gently announces the advent of the divine.

The Gift of Faith in Depression

Into this book are woven many individuals' unique experiences of depression. I honor those who have struggled through the journey to well-being and wholeness against incredible odds, and I am grateful that they have shared with me their stories.[4]

As you read these pages, you may find characteristics or details that hit home and that mesh with your own experience. People who have suffered depression can learn much from each other's stories. Nevertheless, not every experience related here will be completely like yours. You may feel more or less depressed than the people in the stories I have included. You may or may not experience the symptoms narrated here. Be aware, therefore, that flashes of insight or recognition are not a replacement for accurate diagnosis. This book is not intended for self-diagnosis and does not address the more critical needs of those who suffer severe or psychotic cases of depression or bipolar disorder. Rather, it is meant to be a companion as you, or a friend of yours, struggles with his or her dark periods of life. Much in our Catholic tradition and in spirituality can offer strength, comfort, and powerful insight into this struggle. These pages will introduce you to this wealth and be with you as you find God in new ways along this part of your life's journey.

In this second edition, a new part has been added. In these chapters you will find eight steps for inner peace that are rooted in scriptural spirituality, in practical wisdom from living in the present, and in centering prayer. Learning about depression and reading about spirituality are not enough to bring about the changes that we seek in our lives. A step-by-step process will enable those who wish to embark on a journey of personal transformation to more easily find the peace they are looking for.

This book is dedicated to those everywhere who have the courage to walk in the darkness toward the light. I am grateful to Sr. Sean Mayer, FSP, and Sr. Mary Mark Wickenhiser, FSP, of our editorial department, who had the vision, now that the cultural and religious landscape has changed so dramatically, to propose a tenth anniversary updated and expanded edition of *Surviving Depression*. I am honored to have worked with Sr. Mary Lea Hill, FSP, in giving the original text a new shape. Finally, I am conscious that I would not be writing this book if it were not for the support of my community through all the years since my stroke in 1985. Because my sisters did not give up on me, I have the courage to show others suffering from depression the path I found, offering it to them should they find it helpful for their own journey through life.

Ah to tear away once and for all—
to rip my heart out of my breast
and toss to the stars. . . .
This heart so dark and full of
sadness—
this heart so full of alienating pain—
this heart alone against so many feelings—
corrupted by dreams and imaginings—
forsaken by promise and tender words.
So slowly turned to stone . . .
and now this quaking—

the urge to break forth . . .
to soar to the heavens and freedom.
And where will "i" be when
you take sudden flight—
will you take me with you
on your wings of pearl?

Sr. Thomas Halpin, FSP
April 24, 1994

CHAPTER 1

"What's Wrong with Me?"

"I don't want anyone to know I feel this bad, but sometimes I don't even want to get out of bed." *Cheyanne*

≋

"When I was depressed I felt like a non-person, a burden. The darkness engulfed and suffocated everything. Certain few "true" friends who knew and loved me threw out lifelines that I was able to grab hold of. I still prayed even though it seemed useless. But one day Jesus's message shouted through the weltering gloom that he too had experienced the same darkness on the cross. Those last moments were actually the depth of darkness for him, feeling even his Father disowned him. As hard as I tried, I couldn't find life in this inspiration. I couldn't believe that his situation could touch mine. I shared this with a friend and her response was one of those lifelines: 'Well, if you can't believe right now, let me believe for you. Put your trust in my belief that it is true.'" *Anne*

One day a friend shared with me: "Depression was a swirling black hole that sucked me in until I was in well over my head and drowning. The energy needed to fight against it was immense and at times I just let it take over. I was so tired."

I could relate when I heard this. Though my experience of depression had been different, and though each person's symptoms of depression and struggle to survive are unique—it is not difficult to resonate with the story of inner sorrow created by depression when we hear it.

The most difficult thing about taking the first steps toward surviving depression is allowing oneself to *learn* about depression, to stop running, cease the inner chatter by which we try to convince ourselves we are fine, and face the possibility that we may be depressed. In this first chapter I want to lay out simply what depression is, its symptoms and characteristics, the dynamic it creates in our lives. The hardest step, then, will be behind us. The rest of the book can be read with a growing inner peace that opens up the heart to inspiration, courageous insight and resolve, and, above all, to grace.

What Is Depression?

Depression has been called the common cold of mental disorders.

Everyone experiences situations or events in their life that make them sad for a few days, a few weeks, or even a few months. A death, a move, a change of job, graduating from college, or a loss of a pet can be painful and sad, but the feelings are relatively short-lived and not permanent. Depression, on the other hand, interferes with daily life and causes great distress for you and those around you for an extended period of time. Though depression is a common illness, it is a serious one and should be treated with the same care with which you would handle any other medical condition.

Depression affects more than your feelings. It affects your body, mood, thoughts, and the way you feel about yourself. It affects the way you eat and sleep. It influences your perspective on life, on yourself, and regarding others.

What Causes Depression?

Depression is most likely caused by a combination of genetic, biological, environmental, and psychological factors. Depressive illnesses are disorders of the brain. Some theories suggest that neurotransmitters, chemicals that brain cells use to communicate, are out of balance in someone who is suffering from depression. With brain-imaging technologies, such as magnetic resonance imaging (MRI), we can see that the brain of a person suffering from depression looks different from that of a person without depression.

Some types of depression run in families, but those who do not have a family history of depression can become depressed too. Scientists are studying certain genes or combinations of genes that may make some people more prone to depression.

Trauma, loss of a loved one, a difficult relationship, or any other stressful situation may trigger depression. A serious loss, chronic illness, financial problem, or an unexpected and unwelcome change may trigger a depressive episode. The deprivation of love in infancy or one's early formative years, physical or sexual abuse, certain personality traits, and inadequate means of coping can increase the frequency and severity of depressive disorders.

Certain medications used for a variety of medical conditions may cause the onset of depression as a side effect. Specific medications used to treat high blood pressure, cancer, anxiety, and seizures; contraceptives; and some sleep aids can bring about the onset of depression.

National traumatic situations and personal trauma, whether one was directly involved in the incident or watched from afar, can lead to depression. Profound disappointment and scandal can lead to disillusionment and depression.

Personal views we hold about ourselves can also trigger depression. Idealistic people are a gift to the human race. Their ideals and values articulate for the rest of us what we can become. Idealistic people, however, can set themselves up for depression. First, they may never seem able to reach their own ideals—and neither can anyone else—sometimes resulting in cynicism and depression. Second, idealistic people may actually achieve the ideals they have set for themselves, only to find that they must immediately set new and higher ideals to reach. Life becomes an endless chase after utopian dreams.

Because of our high ideals, Christians are sometimes prime targets for depression. High expectations about how to live reinforce ideals that can be unrealistic: *Christians never get angry. Christians never get divorced. Christian families don't have problems. God only loves Christians who are perfect. If we just had enough faith, we wouldn't need antidepressant medication. If we believed in the power of prayer, wouldn't we be happy?* We imagine what the ideal Christian should be and realize that we're not it. But we pretend that we are, sometimes at least. Eventually, however, the knocks of life break this false image of ourselves and we discover that we aren't what Christians "should" be. The tyranny of the image of the perfect Christian leads to its own type of depression, a depression that swirls around the fear that God doesn't love those who don't live up to "my"—not God's—expectations. By confusing God's expectations with our own, we are led to a sense of failure and defeatism.

We expect perfection of ourselves: "God, I thank you that I am not greedy, dishonest, and unfaithful in marriage, like other people" (cf. Lk 18:11). God, instead, extends the gifts of mercy and reconciliation.

Finally, the misunderstanding of others accentuates depression. No one with any sensitivity would expect a person with a broken leg to run a mile or carry a fifty-pound package. It's more difficult, however, to understand and be sensitive to a person who is depressed. People suffering from depression may be afraid to admit they are feeling so low. Admitting this and pursuing counseling or medication would not only expose them to the stigma associated with depression or mental illness, it could also lead to isolation, possible job loss, and family misunderstanding. Often people suffering from depression remain locked in their fears, alone with their anxieties, pretending to be powerful, all the time wishing they could share with someone how badly they feel.

The Unique Experience of Depression

In women. Depression is more common among women than among men. Hormones directly affect the brain chemistry that controls emotions and moods and the hormonal changes associated with giving birth, menstruation, and menopause may be responsible for women being at a greater risk for depression. Women also face the stress of balancing work and home responsibilities, caring for children and aging parents, poverty, and relationship strains—all psychosocial factors that can contribute to a depressive illness in some women. Women who have been the victim of physical, emotional, or sexual abuse, either as a child or as an adult, are vulnerable to developing a depressive disorder. Women with depression have feelings of sadness, worthlessness, and excessive guilt. Women tend to develop depression earlier than men and have depressive episodes that last longer.

In men. Men experience depression differently than women. Men are particularly sensitive to the depressive effects of unemployment, low socioeconomic status, and divorce. They are more likely to be tired, irritable, lose interest in activities that were once pleasurable, and have difficulty sleeping. They may become frustrated, discouraged, angry, and sometimes abusive. Men are also more likely than women to turn to alcohol or drugs, throw themselves into work, or behave recklessly when they are depressed.

In seniors. Seniors show less obvious signs of depression, often causing it to be overlooked. Feelings of grief and sadness can be difficult to distinguish from an ongoing experience of depression. Medical conditions such as heart disease, stroke, or cancer are more prevalent among seniors and may cause symptoms of depression. Medication can have side effects that contribute to depression. Blood vessels, which normally enable good blood flow to the body's organs, including the brain, can become hardened in some older adults, which can contribute to the suffering of depression.

In children. Children who develop depression often continue to have episodes of depression into their adulthood, especially if untreated. Since children are less able to express their feelings in words, they do so with their behavior. Children with depression are difficult to spot because the behavior they exhibit may be viewed as normal mood swings in children. Younger children may pretend to be sick, refuse to go to school, worry that a parent may die, or regress. Older children may sulk, get into trouble at school, be negative and irritable, exhibit persistent boredom, or develop anxiety. Some try to compensate for their low self-esteem by trying to please others by getting good grades and having good relationships with others. Depression in teens comes at a time of great personal change, and it frequently co-occurs with other disorders such as anxiety, eating disorders, or substance abuse. Teens who are depressed may be more likely to take risks, show less concern for their safety, and commit suicide.

How Do I Know If I Am Depressed?

Sometimes it's hard to tell if what one is feeling is, in fact, depression. Through the years, I have picked up books on depression with the secret thought: *Maybe this book will convince me that I really am depressed. Then I will at least know that I am not crazy. . . .* At other times I didn't want information, hoping that the dark feelings inside would keep out of sight long enough so that I could fool myself into thinking everything was going to be okay. Some days I wanted to be able to name and understand the terrible feelings within me, other days I wanted to convince myself they weren't there. People suffering from depression often swing back and forth between being sure they are depressed to being certain they *aren't*, between wanting and *not* wanting to know the truth. How do you know if what you're feeling is depression?

Depression affects our thinking, feelings, behavior, and physical well-being. We may experience problems with concentration and decision-making or we may become increasingly forgetful. Negative thoughts are characteristic of depression. Poor self-esteem, excessive guilt, self-criticism, and pessimism are common. Some people have self-destructive thoughts. Those with depression often feel sad for no reason at all. We lack motivation. We feel lethargic and tired, irritable and angry, and helpless without much explanation. When we are struggling with depression we may withdraw from others and isolate ourselves, eat more or less than normal, and cry excessively. Work and household responsibilities suffer because we don't feel like doing anything. Chronic fatigue, despite more sleep, is common. Some people can't sleep and lay awake for hours at night staring at the ceiling; others sleep most of the day, although they still feel tired. Many lose their appetite, feel restless, and complain of aches and pains.

To begin with, you might ask yourself the following questions:

- ○ Have I become moody, or do I have a significantly strong melancholic mood most of the day, every day?
- ○ Have I lost interest in people and activities?
- ○ Have I gained or lost a significant amount of weight in the recent past?
- ○ Do I have problems falling asleep, or do I wake up unbearably early?
- ○ Do I find that all my thinking is concentrated on surviving the day at hand or with wondering what is wrong with me?
- ○ Do I feel tired all day?
- ○ Do I feel like doing nothing?
- ○ Do I feel little or no energy?
- ○ Do I use drugs, alcohol, pornography, sex, or any other addictive behavior to avoid dealing with reality or to escape my emotions?
- ○ Do I have trouble concentrating?
- ○ Do I see only bad things when I look at myself?

○ Do I have recurring thoughts of death and suicide?

○ Do I feel abnormally restless?

○ Do I cry a lot?

Depression usually carries the stigma of failure. The suggestion by others that one might be feeling depressed is often perceived as an "accusation," a statement about one's inner weakness. "I am not depressed, I'm just down," a depressed person may state, with a stiff upper lip. "I have nothing to be depressed about. How could I have depression?" The person suffering from depression may actually believe that he or she is not depressed. It is hidden from oneself most of all.

Jesus Made Tears Sacred

Persons suffering from depression experience their own vulnerability in a particularly profound way: an experience no one likes, but everyone needs. Jesus made himself vulnerable. He shed tears in his life, died as an apparent failure, left this earth with only a handful of followers who had earlier deserted him. As he hung on the cross, he had only his trust in his Father, the one possession of which nothing could deprive him. Jesus made tears sacred because he cried. He knew the agony and the frustration of our problems. He chose to bear all that is human, and as a man with our human nature he brought us with him on his return to the Father. The One who sits at God's right hand knows what it is to cry. He preached an upside-down world in which the poor, the marginalized, the suffering, those who agonize through emotional pain, are the first, the guests of honor, and the privileged.

The vulnerability of depression doesn't feel holy. It feels like hell. There seems to be no light toward which to walk. There seem to be no options. There often seems no reason to live. Few experiences expose us to our own vulnerability in such a sharp way.

In the winter of 1829, Francis Libermann, a young seminarian studying at Saint Sulpice in Paris, began experiencing excessive fatigue. It became more and more difficult to handle his emotions. Assuming that his studies in theology were wearing him out, he followed his doctor's advice and began to absent himself from his classes in order to take extra time to rest. As the weeks wore on, however, Libermann began to feel increasingly uneasy, as he had a foreboding that there was something seriously wrong with his health.

One day, while visiting another seminarian in the infirmary, a wild shock ripped through his body. Francis fell to the ground in an epileptic fit. When he awoke several hours later, lying on an infirmary bed, Francis felt as if someone had beaten him with clubs. His head throbbed and his eyes were unable to focus. Accustomed as he was to turning to Jesus as his model for life, Francis turned to the Lord to whom he had given his life and prayed, "It is well, O Lord, that you have permitted me to be subject to all this. I am in the midst of torment, but I will not yield to despair."

When the doctor visited Francis, he was surprised to see the young man serene and smiling. Epileptic attacks usually leave their victims feeling gloomy, depressed, and hypersensitive, but the doctor was amazed that the young seminarian exhibited none of these emotional states. Shortly after the doctor left his patient, however, anxiety began to creep into Libermann's thoughts. Panic over whether his condition would force him to give up his dream to be ordained a priest rolled into feelings of morbid guilt and fear that this illness was God's punishment for something he had done. Such floundering back and forth between peace and despair became all-too-familiar to Francis, whose battle with depression lasted the rest of his life.

With time, the epileptic seizures increased. Libermann began to call his mysterious torment "my beloved malady." When he felt engulfed by depression, Francis turned to the chapel or hid in his room, kneeling in prayer, waiting for the black clouds to scatter. He counteracted the anxiety that accompanied the onset of his seizures with a peaceful abandonment to the love of God. Though Francis determined to accept this turn in his health with trust and a peaceful love, the undercurrent in the ocean of his moods was one of loneliness, failure, and discouragement. Once when crossing over a bridge in Paris in the company of another seminarian who was trying to encourage him, Francis stopped abruptly and said: "It is all very well to give these advices when you yourself are happy and peaceful. It is easy to perceive by your tone and by your appearance that you have never passed through such trials. . . . Ah! . . . God grant that life may never be such a burden to you as it is to me."[1] The depression often tempted him to throw himself off a bridge into the Seine River. The dark waters seemed to call to him to finally be done with the misery of his life. The temptation was strong, almost irresistible, and he would have to hurry across the bridge, lest he give in to the siren call of the waters that seemed to promise peace. Francis Libermann once confessed that he never crossed a bridge without the urge to cast himself into the waters below. The uncontrollable urge to end his miserable life was so strong that even in his room he never kept a knife or sharp object within reach.

Eventually his superiors reluctantly dismissed Libermann from the seminary. Francis's suffering, however, made him a master at understanding the struggles and sufferings of others. Gradually, seminarians began coming to him for spiritual guidance, and he became the novice master of the ecclesiastical Society of Jesus and Mary, more commonly known as the Spiritans, founded by John Eudes for the education of priests for the missions. In time, Libermann would gather a group of individuals together to form a small religious community to minister to newly freed slaves in Haiti, Reunion, and Mauritius.

Francis Libermann traveled to Rome in 1838 to request permission to form and direct this new congregation. While there, he had an audience with Pope Gregory XVI, who, upon blessing him, uttered the prophetic words, "*Sará un santo* (he will be a saint)." With Vatican approval, the new congregation was begun, and on Pentecost 1841, Libermann was finally ordained a priest.

Insist on God's Love for You

Libermann had learned that every experience in life, even the most discouraging and defeating, can be the breath of the Spirit, because our sufferings do not define who we are. Francis Libermann is especially suited as a guide for those who suffer depression. He wrote to the Superior of the Convent of the Immaculate Conception (Castres), in August 1843: "Many people are lost through discouragement. This is the universal evil especially among the devout."[2] He encouraged tolerance of those who were struggling, urging gentleness so as to reach and heal the heart of the one suffering depression through encouragement.

Throughout Libermann's life, it was his personal experience of suffering, beginning from his youth, that had made him a gentle and insightful assistant to those who suffered. Today his cause is up for canonization.

Suggestion for prayer

Pray the first sorrowful mystery of the Rosary, the Agony of Jesus in the Garden. Pray this decade of the Rosary gently—one Our Father and ten Hail Marys—and give yourself a chance to stay with Jesus in his sorrow and tears. Enter into Jesus and see, from the inside, what he is feeling as he prays to his Father for help. Then allow Jesus to feel, from the inside, what you are feeling. Listen to what Jesus has to say to you.

For one who is depressed

Make a chart of the factors that could be important to understanding your depression.

Start to write your own story. Note major events, prayer experiences, dreams, inspirations, sudden turns in the road, surprising discoveries.

For a friend

Set aside a few hours every other week just to visit with someone who is depressed. Provide a welcome distraction by bringing over your pet if you have one. Listen and show your understanding. Invite your friend to a movie, take him or her out for ice cream, or go for a walk together.

Some symptoms of depression

- ○ crying
- ○ anger
- ○ weight loss or gain
- ○ fear and anxiety
- ○ violent mood swings
- ○ withdrawal
- ○ irritability
- ○ hopelessness
- ○ feelings of guilt
- ○ oversensitivity
- ○ bursting into tears
- ○ feelings of inadequacy
- ○ change of sleep patterns
- ○ uncontrollable feelings of despair
- ○ no interest in food, or unusual overeating
- ○ apathy
- ○ feeling worthless
- ○ lacking all motivation
- ○ sense of futility

CHAPTER 2

"Will This Last Forever?"

"A year ago I was ready to give up. But then I decided I didn't *want* to give up. The mortgage bank sold the house out from under me. When I was told about it I got a cold chill. But I'm still in the house. No matter what happens I will be fine. I am not going to be homeless. I won't let myself be homeless. A lot has to do with having a positive attitude. I took care of my mom for the last fifteen years of her life. When she was down she always prayed for me to be strong. I learned a lot from her. She was always praying for everybody else, instead of saying 'poor me, poor me.' She was thankful for me and she let me know that. That's how I'm trying to live with this too. I have my life. I have my son. I am grateful for what I do have." *Carmen*

"My husband is fifty-seven and has lost his job. No one will hire him full time. He is working nonstop at odd jobs to make up for lost income. I worry about him. This is a huge pressure on me since I have never worked. I can't get out of my depression." *Kate*

Since 2001 people have experienced emotional trauma, fear, and sorrow in a number of national, ecclesial, and international arenas, contributing to a greater percentage of persons suffering with depression.

I recently met a friend whose brother had died in the attack on the World Trade Center. Ten years later she was still grieving her brother's tragic death. This is a pain that probably time will *not* entirely heal, though my friend may find more joy in her life. We encounter the effects of 9/11 everywhere. They cover a wide gamut from missing family members and friends to yearly memorials, from economic instability resulting in a changed lifestyle to fear of losing jobs and homes. Many have family members and neighbors whose lives have been disrupted by military service in the wars to fight terrorism since 9/11. Veterans of recent wars have come home suffering from physical injuries or post traumatic stress disorder (PTSD). Many people in New York and Washington live with a heightened sense of fear (or anger). Almost everyone viewed the collapse of the towers on television, and according to a study by North Carolina's Research Triangle Institute published in the August 2002 issue of *The Journal of the American Medical Association*, ten million adults in the United States had a friend, family member, or co-worker killed or injured in the attacks. The study also reported that 11 percent of the population of metropolitan New York developed probable PTSD, 30 to 50 percent of the cases probably turning out to be chronic. There is, according to the report, a 4 percent prevalence of probable PTSD as a whole in the country as a direct consequence of the September 11 attacks. A survey of New York City residents conducted after the terrorist attacks by the NIDA-funded researchers Dr. David Vlahov and his colleagues at the New York Academy of Medicine indicates the connection between stress-related symptoms and self-medication with drugs or alcohol to relax or simply to cope.[1]

We all live with a greater sense of anxiety, including lingering uncertainty over our safety, along with the impending possibility of terrorist attacks on planes, on subways, in buildings, virtually anywhere we are. This is evidenced by periodic anthrax-tainted letters, the occasional "shoe bomber," and the constant warnings in subways, airports, and bus terminals to remain vigilant and report anything suspicious. We live in a constant state of unrest.

The terrorist attack on September 11, 2001 has now had ripple effects in countries across the globe that have experienced attacks on their own soil and the breakdown of economic stability. Those who already suffer from depression, or who are psychologically vulnerable in any way, are prone to a greater sensitivity to the changed emotional tenor in the country and may find themselves suffering even more acutely.[2] The National Center for Post Traumatic Stress Disorder states that around the anniversary of tragic events, we can have an "anniversary reaction" that can range from feeling upset for a couple days to experiencing significant psychiatric or medical symptoms.[3]

Besides the trauma of the attack on the United States, there is the ongoing anguish created by economic destabilization and the stress of undergoing foreclosure. The foreclosure crisis has been called a crisis in mental health by Dr. Craig E. Pollack, who, together with Robert Wood Johnson, foundation clinical scholar at Pennsylvania School of Medicine, conducted a study of homeowners whose homes were in foreclosure in Pennsylvania. In their research they reported that nearly half of the people surveyed reported depressive symptoms and 37 percent reported symptoms that indicated probable major depression. Nearly 60 percent had skipped meals and 40 percent hadn't renewed their prescriptions because of the expense. Stress had led to an increase in behaviors that undermine health such as smoking and drinking.

There are other circumstances often associated with the fallout of 9/11 and the subsequent wars that also alter lives and can lead to life-long depression: divorce, a major change in lifestyle as a consequence of the housing or financial crisis, a mental health issue or loss of limb sustained in combat, the excruciating sorrow of a parent who has lost a son or daughter in military service, the strain on spouses raising children alone, as well as their anxiety for the future.

The United States in recent years has also lived through other major tragedies: hurricanes, wildfires, floods, and other natural disasters resulting in widespread property loss and displacement. One only has to think of the 2005 Hurricane Katrina in New Orleans in which 80 percent of the city was submerged by flood waters.

Finally, mention must be made of the clergy sex abuse crisis that broke in Boston in the early spring of 2002 and has since rippled across the globe. It has created a crisis of faith in Catholics who feel disillusioned with their leaders, not to mention the horrific pain and injustice caused to victims, the loss of reputations of those falsely accused, and the shame, loneliness, and discouragement among the majority of the priests who were not involved in the scandal but who have been left holding the pieces.

Heartrending Questions

All of these situations that we have been documenting above remind us of Job in the Bible. The Book of Job begins with a description of the abundant blessings and happiness of Job. He was considered a wise and righteous man. Even the Lord calls attention to his righteousness. Satan, however, tells God that if he were to take away his blessings, God would soon see that Job was not so righteous after all. So God allows Satan to take away Job's wealth, his flocks, even his children. In a second round of bargaining between Satan and God, God allows him to afflict Job with a terrible skin disease. The purpose of this story is to provide an opportunity to deeply meditate on the mystery of suffering, and the narrative strikes a chord in all of us. So, we may ask, does God create suffering? Is God so cavalier with my livelihood and well-being that he can bargain it away to the devil? Is God so cruel that he delights in testing people just to see if they will remain faithful? Are disasters—natural or personal—a punishment from God? Is God trying to say something to me through the tragedies in my life?

Rather than attempt a philosophical or theological answer to these questions that tear at the human heart, I want to cut away to the story of Saint Jane Frances de Chantal. Jane Frances Frémyot de Chantal was born in 1572 in Dijon, France. When she was twenty she married the Baron Christophe de Rabutin-Chantal. When the Baron brought Jane Frances to the Castle of Bourbilly, his young wife found it in great disarray. She immediately set about restoring order in his household and administering his estates. It was a happy marriage, though the couple had to deal with the problem of Christophe's occasional infidelity. Jane reared and educated their three daughters and one son, as well as Claudine de Chantal, Christophe's daughter from another relationship. In 1601 their marriage tragically came to an end when Christophe was mortally wounded while hunting with a friend. Not realizing Christophe had gone into a thicket, his friend fired into the trees, shooting him. Jane was beside herself with sorrow when her husband died in her arms a few days later. He had forgiven his friend and insisted that she do the same.

After her husband's death, Jane Frances went with her children to live with her father-in-law, who was a difficult and unpleasant old man. For seven years she was forced to bear his ill-disposition toward her. Her father-in-law also kept a mistress, adding to the troubles in their relationship. For many years the young widow inconsolably mourned her husband's death, as well as the loss of their beautiful life as husband and wife. Jane de Chantal eventually administered her father-in-law's financial affairs and brought order to his household.

During these dark years, Jane began to sense a call to a new way of life. Her life, like the pieces of a jigsaw puzzle, had been thrown down and no longer fit together as they once had. Desire for something more made her restless, and she began to look for someone to help her. Eventually she found the Archbishop of Geneva, Francis de Sales, who, through many years of patient guidance, helped her discover the secret of what was flowering within her and accept a new vision of life. Together Saint Francis de Sales and Saint Jane Frances de Chantal founded the Congregation of the Visitation of Holy Mary (also known as the Visitation Order). She established over eighty Visitation monasteries before her death.

Resources Within

People who are still suffering from anxiety after 9/11, or who have been displaced by Katrina, or whose homes are in the process of foreclosure, or who suffer from the sex abuse scandals that again and again make headlines in different areas of the world, share with Job and Saint Jane Frances similar feelings: fear, shame, regret, anxiety, guilt, disillusionment, sadness. Universal needs are acutely felt: need for safety, consistency, integrity, balance, security, well-being, health, compassion, and kindness. Job and Saint Jane Frances each discovered that though their lives had changed, though their futures were uncertain, they were not alone. They were still connected to Someone more powerful than they. For both of them the journey through the liminal space of grief and uncertainty brought them to a direct encounter with God. It is after a round of dialogues between Job and his three friends, that God appears to the troubled man.

And the LORD said to Job:
"Shall a faultfinder contend with the Almighty?
Anyone who argues with God must respond."

Then Job answered the LORD:
"See, I am of small account; what shall I answer you?
I lay my hand on my mouth.
I have spoken once, and I will not answer;
twice, but will proceed no further."

Then the LORD answered Job out of the whirlwind:
"Gird up your loins like a man;
I will question you, and you declare to me.
Will you even put me in the wrong?
Will you condemn me that you may be justified?
Have you an arm like God,
and can you thunder with a voice like his?

"Deck yourself with majesty and dignity;
clothe yourself with glory and splendor" (Job 40:1–10).

Then Job answered the LORD:
"I know that you can do all things,

and that no purpose of yours can be thwarted.
'Who is this that hides counsel without knowledge?'
Therefore I have uttered what I did not understand,
    things too wonderful for me, which I did not know.
'Hear, and I will speak;
    I will question you, and you declare to me.'
I had heard of you by the hearing of the ear,
    but now my eye sees you" (Job 42:1–5).

Pain was a process for both Job and Saint Jane: it took time, tears, talking, listening, studying, praying, pleading, and waiting. Eventually both discovered that they had untapped inner resources. Saint Jane, many years after her husband's death, wrote to her nuns: "A soul abandoned completely to Divine Providence desires only God and is detached from all but him: there is no eventuality that can unsettle her. Nothing so strips the soul and gives it greater dependence on God than the practice of the maxim of our blessed Father, Francis de Sales: *Ask for nothing and refuse nothing.*"[4]

Both Job and Saint Jane assumed a new responsibility and capacity for the direction of their lives, and unexpected solutions appeared. In pursuing these transformed horizons, they uncovered inner spiritual depths they hadn't known they had.

A Single Note

Saint Francis de Sales, the friend and spiritual guide of Saint Jane Frances de Chantal commented on Job in these words:

> What I have noticed with doves is that they mourn in the same way that they rejoice, and that they sing always the same note, both in their songs of joy as in the songs in which they lament and express their complaints and sorrow. Whether they be joyous or sad, they never change their tune. Their cooing is ever the same.

It is this holy evenness of spirit which we ought to have. I do not say evenness of humor or of inclination, but of spirit, for we ought to make no account of the fretting of the inferior part of the soul. It is the inferior part of the soul which causes disquietude and caprice when the superior part doesn't do its duty by rendering itself supreme, and doesn't keep a vigilant watch to discern its enemies and be aware of the tumults and assaults raised against it by the inferior part. These tumults spring from our senses and our inclinations and passions to make war upon the reason and to subject reason to their laws. I say, moreover, that we ought always to keep ourselves firm and resolute in the superior part of our soul, to follow virtue and to keep ourselves in a continual evenness amidst events favorable or adverse, in desolation as in consolation.

Holy Job provided us with an example on this subject, for he never sang except in the same key. When God multiplied his property, gave him children, and sent to him at his will everything which he could desire in this life, what did Job say except, blessed be the name of the Lord? It was his canticle of love, which he sang on every occasion. For behold Job reduced to the extremity of affliction. What does he do? He sings his song of lamentation in the same notes which he chanted in his season of joy. "If we have received good things," said he, "at the hand of God, why should we not receive evil? The Lord gave, and the Lord has taken away. Blessed be the name of the Lord." No other canticle, be the time what it may, but this; "Blessed be the name of the Lord."

Oh, how similar was that holy soul to the dove, which rejoices and laments always in the same note! Thus may we do; and on every occasion thus may we receive goods, evils, consolations, afflictions, from the hand of the Lord, ever singing that same sweetest canticle, "Blessed be the holy name of God," and always in continual evenness.

Never let us act like those who weep when consolation fails them, and only sing when it has returned, resembling apes and baboons which are sad and furious when the weather is gloomy and rainy, and never cease leaping and playing when the weather is fair and serene.[5]

～

I remember that you said to me how burdensome you felt the multiplicity of your affairs, and I replied to you that it was an excellent means for the acquisition of true and solid virtue. The multiplicity of affairs is a continual martyrdom. For as the flies weary and annoy those who travel in summer more than the fatigue of the journey itself, so the diversity and multiplicity of affairs give more trouble than the weight of the affairs themselves.

You have need of patience. I hope that God will give it to you if you diligently ask it of him and force yourself to practice it faithfully by preparing yourself for it every morning, by a special application of some point in your meditation, and resolving to settle yourself in patience throughout the course of the day or as often as you feel yourself distracted with business.

Lose no occasion, however trifling, of exercising sweetness of heart toward anyone. Do not reckon on being able to succeed in your affairs by your own industry, but only by the assistance of God. Consequently repose yourself in his bosom, knowing that he will do what is best for you, provided that you use a sweet diligence on your part.

I say a sweet diligence, because there is a kind of violent diligence which perils the heart and the business you transact. Such diligence does not deserve the name, but should rather be called anxiety and trouble. My God! We shall soon be in eternity, and then we shall see what a little matter are all the affairs of the world, and of how small consequence it was whether they were done or not done. Nevertheless, we make ourselves anxious regarding them as though they were great things.

Attend diligently to your affairs, but know that you have no affairs of greater importance than those of your salvation, and the paving of the way to a true and solid devotion. Have patience with all, but principally with yourself. I mean, do not make yourself unhappy about your imperfections, but always have the courage to rise above them. I am very glad that you make a fresh beginning every day. There is no better means for achieving the spiritual life than always to recommence, and never to suppose that you have done enough.[6]

Suggestion for prayer

Light a small votive candle in a glass holder you can safely hold in your hands. As you spend some time in prayer holding the candle, ask God for the grace to find light in the darkness.

———————>୨◉ୡ————————

For one who is depressed

Make a list of what you fear might happen to you, to others, or to your livelihood. Write a letter to God detailing what you have listed. Tell him exactly what you feel and all that you desire. Ask him to send you someone who can help you discover your inner resources and resilience.

For a friend

It is one of the most difficult things to be with, to care about, and to be available to someone who is depressed over a situation that won't immediately change. It is uncomfortable also for the friend because we want to fix the situation. To us this may seem the best way to help the person. But notice in the stories of Job and Saint Jane Frances that God doesn't step in to fix a situation and make the pain go away. God's trust in the capacity of the human heart for resilience and spiritual wisdom would be short-circuited if he played the fix-it game. When you are with your friend, notice your own feelings. Sit with him or her because these feelings, and the deeper needs to which they are connected, are *your* invitation to explore *your* own inner resources and spiritual depth.

————————

Tips for surviving after exposure to personal or national tragedies

Note: Not all of these will be possible for you. Choose one or two that will help you this year.

- ○ Be aware that you may have a strong emotional reaction around the time of an anniversary of the trauma: the date of the attacks, the date of the divorce, the month you lost your job or your house.
- ○ Take care of yourself by eating well, exercising, and getting plenty of rest.
- ○ Talk about your feelings with friends, family, members of your parish, or clergy.
- ○ Seek professional help if you need assistance in dealing with your feelings.
- ○ Be kind to yourself on anniversaries, take some special time for yourself and do something kind for another person in memory of your loved one.

○ Focus on rebuilding yourself and your community.

○ Make time to attend to the needs of others, especially children.

○ Limit your exposure to news reports about the tragic event or ongoing situation.

○ Plan a distraction, such as a picnic, a weekend away, or a visit with friends.

○ Allow yourself to experience feelings of sorrow, sadness, and the sense of loss.

○ Take time to be alone with your thoughts or in prayer.

CHAPTER 3

"No One Understands"

"I don't know why I want to cry. When my friends and I go out to dinner sometimes I tell them how I am feeling. As soon as I start, they say, 'Do we have to listen to that again? Get over it. Everybody has something to deal with.' I just want someone to listen to me." *Cherrie*

❴

"One day a friend said to me, 'You need help; you are depressed.' I will always be grateful to her. I didn't realize I was depressed. Actually, I did not even realize how much I was suffering. I thought everyone felt the way I did. She has continued to be a friend and to stand by me during these years of healing." *Marie*

Just about every depressed person has heard these words in one form or another:

"Everybody has a rainy day."

"Look on the bright side."

"Pull yourself up by your bootstraps."

"That's the way the ball bounces."

"You'll get over it."

"If only you tried harder."

"Just stop and smell the roses."

"It can't be *that* bad."

"Can't you just move on?"

"I'm tired of listening to you tell your story. Can't you talk about something else?"

When a person says these words to another, they may simply be expressing their frustration or fear at not knowing what to do to help someone whom they care about and who is suffering in a way they can't understand. They are in need of assurance that things will get better, information, and connection. When someone who is depressed hears these words, however, they hear accusation and blame. They are in need of understanding, friendship, and care. At a certain point, those who suffer from depression feel that people are thinking these things even if they don't say them. "Maybe they're right. I'm just looking at the dark side of things. If I really wanted to, I'd just shake myself out of this." At times these clichés spark anger.

"If I *could* snap out of this I would!"

"Yes, it *is* this bad!"

"No! There *are* no roses to smell!"

"And for your information, *I didn't stand in line for this!*"

While the depressed person may feel like shouting these words at others, somewhere deep inside there is a fear that what people say is in fact true. "If I just tried harder, *maybe* I could beat this." The fact remains, however, that you *can't* beat depression by willing it away. Depression, like any other medical condition, needs to be addressed seriously. It needs to be dealt with head on. Admitting you have depression is not an expression of defeat. *Not* admitting it is.

When a person is depressed, he or she just wants someone to listen to what is hurting inside. We want someone to see the tears we may not be shedding but long to have wiped away. A black tunnel closes in, snuffing out any flicker of light, and often the only thing a depressed person has left to talk about is the dark tunnel itself. Depression can be so debilitating that it takes up all of a person's attention and energy.

It is true, however, that when conversations center almost exclusively on one's problems, others are eventually turned off. Friends stop calling. When people want a good time, inviting someone who is depressed takes too much emotional energy. And so invitations become less frequent. Little by little, the person suffering from depression finds that they are isolated from others. Friendships imperceptibly unravel as the depressed person retreats into a world that daily becomes more incomprehensible and hopeless. Isolation, a low sense of self-worth, and fear of abandonment thwart any attempt to start new friendships or even revive old ones. Friendship may hold no attraction at all; energy for reaching out to others just isn't there. Friendships built on attraction and shared synergy may seem cruelly out of reach.

If connection, friendship, and intimacy are so important for the person struggling with depression and yet the person herself is cutting off any real possibility for friendships to blossom, what can be done? Frustration can build on the part of those who desire to reach out, as well as on the part of the depressed person who is becoming lonelier. This becomes particularly acute between spouses or in families. Is there a way around this impasse?

Christ Redefined Friendship

Jesus, in his life, death, and resurrection, redefined friendship. For a Christian, friendship is no longer defined by what pleases us or serves our interests, by mere attraction, or by what another person can do for us, but by the gift of self to others. Why? Because this is the way Jesus was a friend to us.

In Christ Jesus, Christians have been called to live in community and worship God together as one body. The Christian community is a model of the loveliness of being chosen as intimate friends with the Lord and each other: friendships that are "lovely" because they are both received and mutually worked at. In the Christian community, the rich live and worship with the poor, the computer geek with the second grader, the sophisticated with the simple, and the CEO with the mechanic. The Christian community is realized when individuals embody the new potential for human nature and the possibility of the graced community that Christ has made possible. Christians are called into a community of persons gathered together not by attraction, but by a call in Christ Jesus, through the power of his Spirit, for the glory of the Father.

Creating a Supportive Network of Friends

"Having someone to talk to on a regular basis is very helpful," Karl believes. "You know they are always there just in case you're really desperate some day and need some help quick!" If you are suffering with depression, friendships may be difficult to cultivate, but they are essential for healing. Start by finding at least five people you can call when you need someone to talk to—people who can count on you for friendship as well. In looking for people who will be part of this support network, seek persons who can empathize with you and listen, who can affirm your individuality and your strengths, and who treat you with love, humor, and honesty. Make sure that in your support network you choose one or two people who could join you for fun activities when you need a good laugh to shake away the darkness. People in your support network should be open-minded and comfortable when you describe how you are feeling and what you want. You will want the kind of person who can accept your ups and downs without being judgmental, yet also help you to move on with their sensitive honesty. Relatives, spouses, soul-friends, therapists, counselors, members of your parish or church community, and neighbors can all be a part of this support network.

After forming a support network, it's a good idea to clarify for yourself how you want others to treat you—and *not* treat you—when you're feeling depressed (or manic). An honest talk with each person about the type of support you need should include freedom for the other person to reflect on whether or not she or he feels able to be there for you in the way you have described. Also, ask questions about *their* preferences. Discuss when they would find it easiest for you to contact them. What things do they like to do? When during the week are they most available to go out for a cup of coffee or a movie? Try to harmonize as much as possible their preferences or possibilities with your needs. Depending on each person's gifts and personality, you might contact one when you need to talk for a few moments on the phone, another when you would like to check out your judgment before making a decision, a third if you need to hand over important decisions for a short period of time, or any of them if you just want someone who can help you laugh.

Perhaps one of your support friends would be willing to give you a ride to Mass on Sunday or pray with you over the phone. Using guided imagery meditations over the phone is particularly effective. I have prayed with friends when they have called and were especially down or felt they were spinning out of control. As we pray together, we picture Jesus in our imaginations. Then I guide them to speak with him and to hand over to him the bundle of their fears or emotional pain. Sometimes I suggest words they can say to Jesus, and often they end up speaking spontaneously to him while we are praying. I conclude by asking them what Jesus is saying to them in response. This sharing in another person's encounter with the Lord is a privileged moment and should always be kept confidential. As I have prayed with others, I have sensed how Jesus calms them, allowing his love to gently heal their worries and fears.

As these relationships of self-gift and availability grow, you will discover little things about the people in your support group. When you're able, send a card on a person's birthday or a holiday. Drop off a special dessert—even if you buy it instead of making it yourself. Try to discover the things they like to do and, when you get together, suggest doing those things first. Notice when they may feel stressed and offer to treat them to coffee, to walk their dog, or e-mail them a message. Such friendships become places of joy and growth for everyone involved. They are filled with the Spirit of Jesus.

Sacrificial Giving and Grateful Receiving

Friendship made a life-changing difference to forty-five-year-old Gail, who lives in Virginia. She was diagnosed with

manic depression when she was nineteen. Gail responded well
to her treatment and was able to lead a productive life. However,
ten years later she was hit by a car and things drastically fell
apart. Her mood swings grew more pronounced, and her family
felt they could not care for her. "My mother was bipolar, so it
was difficult for my parents to deal with my situation. I was living alone and trying to get a job," she remembers. "That whole
period was a terrible time. The medication I had been on was no
longer effective, and I even tried to commit suicide." The miracle of healing that God worked in her life was the miracle of
friendship. "I was pretty desperate," Gail remembers, "so I put
an ad in the paper. Think of a huge city newspaper, and one little
ad on one page, just three lines long. Imagine someone finding
those three lines and calling you up. That's exactly what happened. Ben and I met and eventually married. To me that's the
miracle: God bringing us together. Ben found me and then discovered something in me that he loved. Whether I believed it
was possible or not, he did."

Ben remembers the day Gail told him she was bipolar. "I
hadn't expected that, but the more I thought about it, the more
I realized that it was not a reason to cut off our relationship. By
the time we decided to marry, I had accepted that manic depression was a part of her life."

Gail believes that her illness is much easier to cope with
because of the love that she has received. "He has been the greatest husband for ten years," she says. "He has provided all the
stability I need in my life, all the love I could ever want. In turn
I give him emotional support by just being there for him and
listening." Helping another person enriches your life in ways no
one else sees. "Don't be afraid to develop a relationship with
someone who may be suffering from depression," Ben says.
"Having a relationship has helped both Gail and me greatly.

Being together and being in love with each other has made life more beautiful for both of us."

Friendships founded on sacrificial giving and grateful receiving—on the part of both persons—increase love in the world. Having a meaning larger than oneself can help a person suffering from depression to take a step toward connection and presence. More often than not, others are just waiting for you to ask them to be a part of your life. In a deeply Christian way, these people become intimate friends because their friendship transcends mutual attraction and interest. We can become a sacrament of Christ's presence for each other, a Eucharistic reality through the element of self-gift that characterizes these supportive relationships.

The Liturgy: A School of Remembering God's Faithfulness

The Eucharistic liturgy brings the reality in our lives into contact with God's sensitive love and passion to save. The liturgy of the Eucharist is the only place that can hold both the tension of sorrow and the exuberance of praise. Sorrow without praise is deadening; praise that does not encounter sorrow is a hollow experience. In the rites and the prayers of the liturgy, in its readings and doxologies, we discover who we are, but also, and primarily, we discover who God is for us. In the reassuring repetition of rites and prayers, we are taught and shaped by the story of God's intervention in our lives.

In the liturgy of the Eucharist, the sorrow and pain of disobedience and human vulnerability meet the aching love of a God who will not let his people die. We too are caught up in this Eucharistic work of Jesus, the divine Good Samaritan who served his creatures, washed his apostles' feet, and who tends to all our wounds in the liturgy. The relationships you cultivate among the members of your support team or with those who share with you the sorrows and struggles of your depression are just such "Good Samaritan" relationships, extending the Eucharistic presence of Jesus, Servant and Samaritan, in the world today.

What I receive from the Eucharistic liturgy doesn't depend on how I feel or whether I have a "good experience" at Mass. It is rather about what *God* has done, and all that God promises to do. As Catholics, our daily lives are not fully broken open until they are joined with others in this art of praising and thanking God in the midst of our human situation. To pray *for* and *with* and *out* of a suffering world, out of our own suffering is to learn something true about praise and blessing; it is to profess most authentically that God is God, the One who alone deserves our worship and adoration. To continue to worship in the liturgy, to acknowledge God in the midst of adversity as well as in good fortune, is to understand ever more deeply who we are in relation to God. The liturgy is best celebrated when we bring real life to the healing and consoling, the reconciling and illuminating work of God. There we learn to speak the language we pray. We are refashioned and our perspectives enlightened through the repeated hymns of praise and thanksgiving, our voices raised with the angels in the proclamation of the power of God's love: *Holy, Holy, Holy Lord God of hosts.*

The liturgy is a school for remembering who God *has* promised to be, and by recalling who God has been for us, we can then know who God *will* be. And we can remind God to be God—to come and save us *now*!

Suggestion for prayer

Using an old missalette, and in a quiet moment, take a pen and underline in the Order of the Mass the statements about what God has done for us. Circle the words: *praise, thanksgiving,* and *joy.* Read some of the Scripture readings and underline the words that express the human situation in all of its drama and complexity. Use this missalette at Mass to enter more deeply into the mystery of the liturgy where God holds and heals us in power and love.

―――――⟩⊙⟨―――――

For one who is depressed

Make a list of five people you could ask to be part of your support team. Write down for yourself what you would like to ask of them.

After contacting these people, begin to network with them, creating a team of people who can offer you assistance and friendship when you need it.

For a friend

Notice if you find yourself using clichés with your friend who suffers from depression. If so, try asking instead, "Can you tell me what it's like for you?" At times, include him or her in your recreational activities.

―――――⟩⊙⟨―――――

Suggestions for support

(Not all of these are helpful or possible for everyone all the time. Choose those best suited for you at this time.)

- ○ Talk with a good friend.
- ○ Reach out to help someone.
- ○ Go to a support group.
- ○ Do a hobby with someone.
- ○ Arrange to be around others.
- ○ Spend time with a pet.
- ○ Go to Mass with a friend.
- ○ Go for a walk with someone.
- ○ Call a crisis clinic or hotline.
- ○ Exercise with someone.
- ○ Join a parish committee with a friend.
- ○ Chat with a family member.
- ○ Spend time with good friends.
- ○ Let yourself be held by someone you love.
- ○ Talk with someone in your parish.
- ○ Pray.
- ○ Choose to be around people who don't criticize, judge, or want to change you, but who accept you for who you are at this point in your life.
- ○ Be okay with who you are, not trying to live up to another's expectations.

CHAPTER 4

"Why Doesn't God Heal Me?"

"In the last fifteen years, I have struggled with periods of depression several times. The first time I was seriously depressed, I went for therapy and worked through my memories of trauma and repressed feelings. The second time I became depressed, I was surprised. I thought that I had done that work 'once and for all.' I prayed about this. Actually, I prayed rather desperately. Looking back, I realize that I felt like a failure, as though I did not get it 'right' the first time. God gradually revealed to me that all of this is an important part of my life's spiritual journey. Each time I worked through my issues and my past, it was at a deeper level and I became healthier and more integrated. I became aware that each time I struggled with depression my relationship with God changed. I was able to trust God more. Actually, all of my relationships changed: with myself and with others." *Pat*

Depression affects a person's thoughts, mood, feelings, behavior, and overall health. No scientific terminology can capture the degree of pain experienced by those who suffer from it.

Dreams previously clung to seem to vanish overnight; beauty that once gave inspiration no longer exists. Instead, a person's mind may be filled with negative thoughts such as: *I have failed. I have no value. My views are worthless. All this is my fault. I don't know what is happening to me. Why do I feel this way? I've asked God to help me. Why doesn't he do something?*

Those of us who struggle with depression usually wonder why God doesn't do something to help us. Praying for a miracle is often our last hope for help. Since we feel we can't do anything ourselves, we hope that God can. When God doesn't work the expected miracle, we wonder if God even notices us or cares about what is happening to us. Or perhaps we think God is punishing us for past failures. However, God doesn't usually deal with us by arresting the forces of nature and miraculously healing us. When a physical miracle is all we're hoping for, God can seem to be uninterested in our plight or to have decided that for some mysterious reason we should suffer. God sees the "big picture"—the context in which the depression has occurred—and often works to heal us, others, and the very situations in which we find ourselves in ways that are beyond our imagining. This requires the tremendous risk of opening up, of letting go of our own plans and projects to get on with our life.

Leaving Behind My Attempts to Fix Depression

In my own experience of depression, I had to learn to acknowledge my helplessness. All my attempts to fix my depression were just that—*my* attempts. I had managed to get my life back on track by controlling my feelings with my mind—intellectualizing instead of feeling. I understood the causes of my depression, put into practice what was suggested, and moved on. I knew—rather than felt—how it was tearing my life apart. I figured out what I needed to do to get better. I became an expert at analysis and self-diagnosis. I set about doing everything I was supposed to do. Yes, *I* did it. Everything should have worked. And it did! Well, it did and it *didn't*. It was as if I needed surgery, but all I could do on my own, without a surgeon, was take vitamins. The "vitamins" definitely helped. For seventeen years, they made my life more manageable and calm. But without "surgery," I remained on the level of coping. In reality, I needed not just any surgeon, I needed the Divine Physician.

Over several days of prayer, the Divine Physician took me under his care. Every year we Daughters of Saint Paul make a weeklong silent retreat. These days are set aside exclusively for prayer. I had arrived at the retreat house without any particular expectations. However, immediately upon beginning the retreat I found myself desiring to pray with Jesus in his passion, death, and resurrection, using the passion narrative from the Gospel of John (chapters 18–21).

The scene came alive in my imagination and my heart. I saw Jesus standing before Pontius Pilate and his accusers, one silent, sad, beaten man in the midst of a loud and raucous crowd. *How could Jesus stand there*, I wondered, *while everyone around him was calling for his death. How could he be so calm?*

As I placed myself in the crowd, listening to what was being said, and to the noise and the anger, I could feel Jesus's calmness, a silent space of peace in the midst of everything around me. I began to hear Jesus saying quietly to the crowd, "Yes. Take me. Do what you want with me. My death will be your salvation." I could see the Father hugging him tightly. "Give yourself over to them," God told his Son. "I can never let you go, no matter what happens. I am with you. You are safe in my arms." After a long period of prayer, I realized that the Father was within me as he was within Jesus. He was also holding me and assuring me, "Do not be afraid. You are safe in my arms."

On another day, I contemplated Jesus right after Pilate had condemned him to death and washed his hands of any personal responsibility. I saw Jesus dragged off by those who had called for his death. The moment of terror I felt, as his final walk through Jerusalem began, was excruciating. I prayed for many hours, holding that terror in my heart, desiring to comfort Jesus, to tell him I was there for him and that I would not leave him alone.

One day in prayer, I stood beneath the cross and sank to the ground at its foot after he had died. I had promised Jesus I would not leave him alone, and so I stayed there keeping watch. I kept the cross before my eyes for hours, feeling the sorrow Mary must have felt, as I asked for the courage to stay near her Son. It was at this point my retreat director pointed out to me that perhaps God was bringing together Jesus's experience and my own. I wasn't sure what he meant, but as I left our meeting and returned to the chapel, I began to cry. For several hours, in prayer before the Eucharist, scenes of my hospital stay after my stroke so many years before alternated with scenes of Jesus's passion and death. It was like watching a movie. My moments of loneliness and fear alternated with his loneliness and fear. I cried quietly—seventeen years worth of tears. God truly was embracing me tightly and saying, "Do not be afraid even of this. I am holding you tightly and nothing can hurt you."

These cleansing tears began a process of healing, a miracle of God's love for me as I began to pray over my "passion." Just as I, in that prayer, had remained beneath the cross after Jesus had died, I now sensed Jesus sitting on the floor at the foot of my hospital bed keeping *me* company. As I had stayed with Jesus through his passion, he now kept watch with me. The many lonely years of struggling with the consequences of my stroke and the resulting bipolar disorder were "healed" in this prayer. God did not miraculously heal me of temporal lobe epilepsy. Instead, I began to see that I had been keeping myself at a sufficient distance from God to protect myself from anything else God could "do" to me. I had been afraid of God, trying to build my own life without him where it was safer. God nevertheless had waited until the right moment to enter once again into my life and turn me toward him. I did not receive the physical healing I had wanted. I received something better.

God never promised that we would live free from all suffering. God promised that nothing could ever remove us from his love and care, or, as a therapist of mine once put it, "Don't be afraid of the worst that could happen to you. It will, *but it doesn't matter!*" While I couldn't put into words what I felt the first time I heard those words, I instinctively knew them to be true.

Jeanne, a friend, once shared with me her struggle with trusting God while she was in therapy for depression that could be traced back in part to early traumatic experiences. "One day when I was talking to God about the time that I had been sexually abused, I angrily cried out to Jesus, 'Where were you when he did this to me?' In my heart, I heard Jesus respond, 'I was with you, crying.' As I continued in prayer, I understood that Jesus had been there with me during the abuse and that he had hated to see me hurt. But I also understood that he continued to be with me as I worked through the memories, enlightening me, strengthening me, giving me courage, and healing me."

Meeting Jesus in a Sacrament of Healing

Although not a prolonged experience like a retreat, the sacrament of Reconciliation is a privileged and easily accessible encounter with Jesus the Healer. Today many people don't have a life-giving experience of this sacrament. Laundry lists of sin, shame, boredom, or a sense of the futility of it all sometimes shroud the radiance of God's mercy that flows to us in confession. People will more willingly air their most personal sins on talk shows before they will speak to Jesus through the priest in the secrecy of this sacrament. Therapists, counselors, and support groups make much more sense to a psychologized and theologically impoverished generation.

Therapists are indeed wonderful assets on the road to health, and sometimes they are indispensable. Sharing your experience of depression with a friend can be helpful too. However, the sacrament of Reconciliation offers a particular space of encounter with God, the Church, and ourselves that cannot be duplicated elsewhere.

In the sacrament of Reconciliation, Jesus enters into our inner darkness, confusion, and sin with immense tenderness and love. Rather than bringing a list of sins, I've found it is most important to bring *myself* to this meeting with Jesus in confession. This is particularly true for those who are struggling with the confusion and darkness of depression. Why? The psychological complexity, overbearing sadness, frustration, guilt, and sense of loss that accompany depression can skew our own vision of who we are and how we can most truly live our baptismal dignity. For example, we can mistake severe depression for loss of faith or the irritability characteristic of the illness for a sin of impatience. We see symptoms of our illness as enormous failures in responding to God. The sacrament of Reconciliation is a place to bring all of our chaos into contact with the healing love of the Lord Jesus. How can you do this?

First, if possible, choose one priest with whom you feel comfortable celebrating the sacrament. When you have found a priest you feel you can trust, ask him if you could make an appointment for Reconciliation once a month or so (or arrange your schedule to match the confession schedule of the parish). Second, gradually share with him pertinent information about your diagnosis or what you are going through, providing him a context for understanding what you bring before the Lord in the sacrament. Third, tell the priest what makes you feel guilty. As mentioned, those who suffer with depression or other emotional problems can find it difficult to distinguish between sin and the power of disorderly emotions. Depression can distort our vision of self. In the sacrament of Reconciliation, with the help of an honest conversation with the priest, you can get God's perspective on your life.

It is very helpful to return to the same priest to celebrate this sacrament because he will better understand your particular difficulties and circumstances. I used to go to confession to various priests, but the particular difficulties I experienced as a direct consequence of depression were often misunderstood because they did not know me or my story. I received widely differing advice, some less helpful than others, because the priests had no context in which to understand what I said. When I found a priest whom I could trust to understand my situation, I was able to share my story, my struggles, and my day-to-day attempts to live according to the Gospel. Once I learned from him how to distinguish the effects of depression from sin, I was able to experience the compassion the Lord had for me. My confessor was able to help me discover how God was acting in my life, and, as he helped me to accept my struggle with depression for what it was, I began to feel awed by God's presence and gentle healing. The efficacy of the sacrament does not depend on the advice of the priest. However, the conversations that happen within the celebration of the sacrament help shape our conscience and form our image of God and ourselves. Through the regular celebration of this sacrament we become more sensitive to the way God truly is loving us, caring for us, and desiring our good. We gradually learn to walk, and then to run in the ways of true happiness and joy.

The regular celebration of Reconciliation while working through personal issues with a therapist or counselor can bring the gentle, healing gift of grace that will gradually bring us to the point of being able to forgive those who may have contributed to the onset of depression in our lives, an essential element to acquiring emotional health.

What a relief it is to know that it's not all up to us! We can connect to the Church, to the community of believers, to Jesus's mercy through the sacrament of Reconciliation, the sacrament of healing. We can count on God standing with us and for us in our journey toward well-being.

We Can Trust the Healing Process

Even when it is impossible to feel that we believe in anything at all, miraculously God is *still* healing us. Generally healing will be gradual. It is rarely dramatic. Frequently it comes under the simple gesture of one person reaching out to another. In unexpected places, and through unsuspecting people, God comes into our lives. Through one person's illness, God may heal another person who offers to help. One person's journey of healing may be another person's salvation. Or, through a person's depression, God may help the sufferer discover a deeper meaning in life. It is all mystery. It is all sacred, holy ground.

We may not be able to see evidence of God's presence in our lives. Depression in severe cases, and particularly depression in those who have been abused, is often filled with a terrible sense of isolation, of being "evil," of the belief that the anguish they feel is a punishment from God. Nevertheless, it is absolutely reliable and undeniably certain that God is laboring within everyone and everything for our good and our salvation. God holds us tightly. He will never let us go. Healing is a process. It takes time. But we can trust the process no matter how long it takes. Nothing is ever a detour in our lives because every road leads us into God's embrace.

Healing can begin after we admit that we cannot fix ourselves. We need to say yes to our powerlessness and stop demanding miracles on our own terms. When we demand things of God, we keep running away from where we are and, in so doing, we do not allow ourselves to be held by the only One who can heal us.

Suggestion for prayer

Here is a summary of the sacrament of Reconciliation if you would like to celebrate this gift of God's mercy:

Prepare. Take some time to prayerfully recall positive moments of light, grace, unexpected goodness, and peace in your life since your last confession. What do these moments say to you? Be concrete, write it down. Then reflect upon what is troubling you about your life. Are there choices, ways of reasoning, behaviors, or desires that directly weaken your relationship with God, the Church, others, or yourself? Are there aspects of your life that make you sad, confused, or frustrated that you would like to bring before the Lord? In what ways has God blessed you or how have you grown since your last confession?

Make an appointment to celebrate the sacrament. Phone your parish to speak with a priest, speak with a priest you know, or go to confession at the time scheduled in your parish.

Know that you are welcome. You and the priest may greet each other. The priest may urge you to have confidence in God. If the priest is your regular confessor, you might want to say anything that you would like him to know.

Confess your sins. Let the priest know your sins. You can take this time to discuss difficulties you are having, for example, "Father, I know I should be much more loving to my children, but with this new medicine I am taking, I barely get any sleep at night. I am so tired. Nevertheless, I want to bring before the Lord my sorrow at not being able to be there more for my children during these weeks and ask God for the strength to grow in love and patience, as well as in gratitude to my husband who has been extra patient with me." The priest may speak with you about what you have said.

Receive your penance. The priest will recommend a prayer or an action you can do to indicate the sincerity of your sorrow. If it sounds too difficult, let him know.

Pray for forgiveness. The priest will invite you to say a prayer of sorrow aloud. You can pray a traditional prayer of sorrow or speak to God in your own words.

Receive absolution. The priest proclaims the words of absolution and God forgives your sins.

Conclude. The priest may say, "Give thanks to the Lord for he is good." If so, answer, "His mercy endures for ever." Or, he may conclude informally.

As soon as possible after your confession, complete the penance the priest has given you.

For one who is depressed

Write down a history of your depression, looking especially for the little miracles along the way that show God's presence and care. These might be people who came into your life, experiences you have had, an answer to a prayer, information or treatment that gave you a new understanding of your illness, reconciliation with a friend or family member, or an especially strong awareness of God's presence.

For a friend

The sacrament of Reconciliation can also be a privileged space for you as a friend of someone suffering from depression. By sharing the ins and outs, the difficulties and struggles of such a friendship, the sacrament can become a place where real growth in love and self-giving can occur. Share the context of your struggles and limitations (you needn't share names), as well as where you feel you have been self-serving rather than self-giving with your friend. Reconciliation is a graced moment in which you can bring before the Lord your joys and desires, your struggles and weaknesses, a place where God can re-create you little by little as a friend after his own heart.

Basics for surviving depression

- Get eight to ten hours of sleep each night. Don't stay in bed longer or cut your sleep shorter.

○ Take a walk between 11:00 AM and 2:00 PM. The bright light has an antidepressant effect. Sunlight triggers the production of an endogenous form of vitamin D that is anti-inflammatory and helps prevent stress.

○ Abstain from the use of alcohol and street drugs, both of which induce depression and prevent antidepressants from working effectively.

○ Eat a well-balanced diet.

○ Create a schedule for yourself.

○ Take medication as prescribed.

○ Avoid the use of products that contain aspartame. Studies have shown that these products can increase a person's depression if he or she is already depressed.

○ Balance your omegas. The ideal balance between omega-6 and omega-3 fats is one-to-one.

○ Take part in engaging hobbies and activities with other people.

○ Get a bird or another easy-to-care-for pet. A pet provides company and can also be a conversation starter when talking with friends.

○ Choose a friend that you can check in with every day. A depressed person can find it difficult to get out of a rut or a destructive pattern of thinking. Even a phone conversation lasting just a few minutes can be sufficient to help you see a different perspective. A consistent phone call "appointment" can punctuate the "forever" feeling of depression.

○ Daily exercise, even as simple as a brisk walk, will give you more energy. Studies show that ninety minutes of exercise a week can be as effective as some psych-medicines.

○ Keep a journal.

○ Develop a global framework, a way of understanding the world through a larger lens, such as a religious, philosophical, or scientific worldview. Those who have a global perspective on life seem to have an increased resilience when it comes to maintaining mental health.

Chapter 5

"How Do I Start?"

"The only person who can choose to live your life is you. You must decide for yourself that you want to deal with the pain."
Ruth

"One Good Friday, I was particularly tried by mental anguish and struggled with these thoughts. I was close to despair. Then, all of a sudden, I heard Jesus say, 'You are sharing in my mental sufferings during the Passion.' I felt suddenly at peace and made an act of abandonment to God and again tried to accept my illness." *Linda*

I met Leanne, a colleague at Weston Jesuit School of Theology, on the day of our graduation. She was such a gentle and spiritual person that I would have never guessed the struggles she had been through in the past three years, except for a few hints she let slip here and there in our conversation. She said briefly that her husband had divorced her during her time of studies at Weston, and that the presence of her three teenage

children at the graduation Mass and ceremony was very mean-
ingful to her.

Facing the end of my twenty-two year marriage, raising three
teenagers in the face of a loss that has changed their lives
forever, dealing with serious physical problems (I had two
major surgeries in the same year), and struggling through
theology school brought about significant issues of depression for me.

The high achieving perfectionist part of my personality
has somehow always been "held in check" by the other extreme
of my personality: the caregiver. I just can't do it well enough
for myself, and I just can't give enough to others. Addressing
my new life-struggles involved surrender in order to realize
that help was needed for a lady in search of a new identity,
someone who was lost in the depths of perfection, care giving,
and loving everyone . . . except herself.

One day following my second surgery, I can remember
lying on the living room floor, feeling extremely helpless. I was
hurting inside and out. My hip was sore from surgery and my
heart was sore from isolation and physical immobility. Only
the year before, I had run seven miles every day. Now here I
was lying down and looking across the room at the crutches I
knew I would be depending on for a long time. My mother
was there to help me and without her unyielding support, I
don't think I would have made it. The presence in the room on
that particular day was marked by a very special peace, in spite
of the pain. I began to cry. Mom said to me, "It is time that you
got some emotional help." She paused for a moment and
added, "You have been in physical pain for nearly a year now,
your husband is verbally abusing you, you have three children
who love you very much and who are hurting more than you
can know. Leanne, you are special, and you can get through
this. You can get the help that you really want and that you
really need."

I got up and called my primary care physician for the
name of some psychotherapists. He gave me a list of names,

one of whom was his wife. He told me she was a deeply spiritual person and that I should contact her. I immediately called her, and my journey began.

When I started therapy, I also sought spiritual direction. This involved a weekly commitment to the spiritual exercises of Saint Ignatius. The priest who was my spiritual director was extremely helpful in guiding me through a way of praying that encouraged me to *ask* God for hope and healing. You see, I never felt worthy to ask God to rid me of my pain.

My therapist helped me to unravel a journey that had begun with my sister's death when I was just five years old. Carrying the blame for her failure to beat her cancer was something I had never let go of. For many years, I had felt that there had to have been something more I could have done to *save her*. Naturally, I had grown up with the sincere notion that I had to keep everyone I loved from dealing with any pain or suffering. With these roots securely in place, I had much to do to give myself permission to experience and work through the grief I had stored up within me. Among many other things, I had to free myself from the burden of my sister's death.

I also began to understand that depression develops when people don't have a true sense of who they are and what they are about. There was no such thing as self-identity in my book. . . .

For two years I worked with my therapist and my spiritual director. I felt blessed that both appreciated and respected their role in my healing process. Medically, I remained committed to physical therapy, exercise, and a very mild dose of Prozac. The pain came and went. I stood up and made it through very trying days. I also fell down and crashed many times over, only to get up again, stronger and more determined to run this race.

I gave myself the gift of a support network of loving friends, my pastor, and my professors. People watched me make my way and reached out to me in many more ways than I could have imagined. Most importantly, I learned to accept their love and their support. In the end, I was able to learn who I am, what it is that I am all about, and that I must love myself more and more and more.

My relationship with God grew deeper and deeper. The intimate presence of God through my difficult days taught me about suffering. I learned to pray in such a way that I gradually realized how close God was to me. I learned to trust, to surrender, to hope, and to love. I learned that I was "on the journey" upward, that I was making my ascent toward God—a God of hope, healing, and love.

If you, like Leanne, have suffered from depression long enough or know someone who has, then you know how insurmountable the obstacles to emotional well-being seem. This chapter is about the first steps you can take.

Educate Yourself

Find out all you can about mood disorders. Go online and do research. Read books. Ask questions of your doctor. Take self-tests that you can find online or in books. While none of these sources will be comprehensive or even enough for an accurate diagnosis, all knowledge gained empowers you to make more informed decisions. You will have to make many choices during your journey to wellness, including choices about treatment options, lifestyle modifications, career assessments, relationships, living space, and leisure.

You may discover that your frustration with a career choice is adding to your depression and a new path may open up to you. If you are a parent, you may also find yourself rethinking your parenting style. A destructive relationship or particularly unhealthy eating habits may contribute to your depression. The more you know about mood disorders and their causes, the more you can become an active protagonist in your own treatment.

First Things First

The first step toward surviving depression is generally the same for everyone. Have a complete physical examination with a physician you trust. Make follow-up appointments for any other specialists to whom you are referred. Ask that copies of all your medical records from follow-up appointments be referred to the physician who did the initial physical examination. If you are not getting answers that help explain what you are feeling, pursue appointments with doctors who are specifically trained in psychological or neurological issues. I learned the hard way that follow-up was important. Because I had had a stroke, I pursued follow-up appointments through the years simply with a neurologist. The conclusion of the check-ups was always a clean bill of health until my emotional distress was so acute I was referred to a psychologist. This was helpful in addressing underlying issues that were contributing to my mood swings. However, after moving away from my therapist my mood swings became more pronounced and the rapid cycling in the end brought me close to a breakdown. After an exam by a neuro-psychiatrist trained in both neurology and psychiatry, I was referred to the department of cognitive neurology in a nearby hospital that correctly diagnosed my condition and started treatment that finally addressed the physiological components of my situation. It is important, if at all possible, to have a complete exam at the outset of determining treatment. If treatment suggestions do not seem to bring about results, then pursue assessment with doctors in more specialized fields.

Conflicting diagnoses for depression or mood disorders are common. For example, when Tye was diagnosed by a psychiatrist as having a slight mood disorder, he began taking the prescribed medication. Though he went ahead with the medication for several months while meeting with his psychiatrist weekly, something just didn't seem right to him. He didn't find his sessions helpful and was unsatisfied with the medication he was taking, but the doctor was unwilling to explore other possibilities. After almost a year, Tye decided to get another opinion. The new doctor was able to pinpoint the type of depression he was suffering from and prescribed a different medication. Within weeks, Tye began to feel good again.

Learning all you can about mood disorders and insisting that you get the appropriate testing is essential for correct treatment. If cost is a problem, other payment options are available. Consult your local hospital or ask your doctor for information.

Commit Yourself to the Process

As a person is diagnosed and treatment begins, two things can happen. First, a person may start to feel better quickly, and as a result cut short the continued investigation of possibilities that such disorders generally require. I have seen this happen so often. I know someone whose general practitioner prescribed a medication for depression and encouraged him to see a psychologist or counselor. Since he felt so good immediately after beginning his medication, he never made an appointment with a psychologist, but continued taking the medication. Several years later, friends who noted his mood swings encouraged him once more to see a psychologist. After appropriate testing, it became evident that while he felt "wonderful," the prescribed medication was contributing to his increasing emotional instability. He was placed on a small dosage of another medication and began therapy to resolve underlying issues.

The second common situation I've seen is that some people, after giving their doctor one—and only one—chance to "make them feel better," decide to switch doctors without bringing their history with them. Geri, a woman I've known for many years now, had been to four or five different doctors before I met her. If she decided that she didn't trust what one doctor was telling her, she went on to another. Each of the successive doctors did not know her history, and, therefore, none of them were able to get to the source of her problems. After you find a doctor you are comfortable with, give him or her a chance to help you. It will take many tests and seemingly "false starts" to narrow down what exactly is at the root of the problems you are experiencing. Keep your own record of appointments, tests you have had, doctors' recommendations, medications you have been prescribed, any reactions, etc. Although when you see a new doctor you should insist that your medical records be sent to him or her, documenting your own medical situation will be very valuable.

The journey to wellness may take years. After a correct diagnosis, the search for the right medication begins. There are many drugs on the market that can be used for safely treating depression. Your doctor will discuss these with you. Be sure to ask about possible side effects. Once you begin medication, it's important to share with your doctor any reactions or difficulties you experience. Usually you will begin to have an indication of how the medication is helping with your mood disorder after two or three weeks. Don't be embarrassed to keep informing your doctor how you feel. In the end, you should be feeling good. Don't be satisfied with less. The doctor may need to change the dosage or prescription, add another medication, or recommend therapy, behavioral or lifestyle changes, or diet modification. Many aspects of your treatment will need to be balanced to attain emotional well-being. Be patient and work with your doctor. Your treatment will be as unique as you are.

Don't Leave It All to Medication

Medication is not always the whole answer. Twenty-year-old Ruth, presently studying social work at a large Catholic university, was prescribed appropriate medication for her depression and began counseling. As time went on, Ruth's symptoms grew less severe and continued decreasing. Now, five years after having begun treatment, Ruth no longer needs medication. Her program for wholeness included some time on medication, regular counseling, lifestyle modification, and behavior changes, along with daily participation in the Eucharistic celebration. Although medication may be a large part of your treatment, there are many issues related to your depression that can't be "medicated" away. After my doctor had tried combinations of several medications, he suggested therapy, for at least a short period, so that he could determine what other issues were involved in my depression. Through therapy, I was able to identify some of these issues and work to resolve them. Consequently I was able to minimize the medication I needed. Some time later I again started working with a social worker at the cognitive neurology unit who was trained in supporting people who had suffered neurological incidents. She was extremely helpful in showing me how to put into place practical arrangements that could help me function with greater ease.

One blessing of struggling with depression for me has been a lifelong passion for self-improvement and spirituality. Recently I discovered a group that teaches and practices nonviolent communication.[1] I meet with Pat, my coach, every couple of weeks. We review conversations I have had, or am preparing for, in order to understand my feelings and needs as well as the feelings and needs the other person might experience. We role-play conversations. This regular connection with my own feelings and needs and a growing capacity to appreciate those of others, while letting go of blame, has contributed to my having experienced a greater sense of peace and ease in my relations with others and in my daily work. I encourage you to pursue opportunities in self-development because each opportunity, and all of them together, contribute to inner freedom and the capacity for emotional growth.

Some recommendations to consider when choosing a therapist: try to find someone who has extensive experience and knowledge of your type of illness. If you are seriously depressed or bipolar, make sure that the therapist has a backup when on vacation or otherwise unavailable. In your first interviews, see if the therapist communicates an attitude of caring and interest. You can find good therapists often through the referral of doctors or friends, through mental health organizations, or through your psychiatrist. Your parish office might also be able to give you a recommendation of a Catholic therapist in your vicinity.

It takes enormous courage to commit to therapy or counseling. When you give yourself fully to the process and you begin to explore your issues, it can seem that things get worse before they get better. It's important to tell your therapist how you think things are going. If you think that things are going well, say so, but also be frank if you think your therapist is making connections or drawing conclusions that do not make sense to you. If you think you and your therapist aren't working well together, let him or her know. The key is to explore these issues with the therapist and not make snap decisions on your own. *You* have to claim responsibility for your journey to well-being, but work with your therapist.

Consider Joining a Support Group

The people who best understand depression or bipolar mood swings are people who have been or who are depressed or bipolar themselves. It can be healing to be with people who have similar problems. In a support group, you don't need to hide your problems. People there understand. Support groups can also be a good source of information on mood disorders and tips for handling problems associated with mood swings.

To locate support groups in your area, call your local mental health help line or contact local mental health facilities. Not all support groups are the same. If one doesn't meet your needs, you might try exploring another. Make sure you join a support group that is constructive for you.

The Church as Spiritual Hospital

The journey to emotional health and wholeness is not restricted entirely to the sphere of psychology. In Eastern Orthodox spirituality, writers such as Saint Gregory of Nyssa (335–395), Saint Gregory Palamas (1296–1359), and Saint John of Sinai (c. 579–649), among others, believed that illnesses of the human psyche and heart are best addressed by theology. Saint John of Sinai, for instance, saw the journey to wholeness as a journey from isolated individuality toward a relationship with God, with the community, with oneself, and with all of creation. Because the "cure" for someone suffering from depression or other illnesses is a journey from an inward love to a love that reaches out to God and others, these Christians believed that this process needs to take place in a spiritual climate. They saw the Church as a spiritual hospital.

Today we live in a society that fosters individualism, a society in which people are separated from each other and the possibility of community and communion. Even many parish communities have lost much of their communal nature. A friend of mine who was living through the hell of her husband's arrest found herself slipping in and out of the Eucharistic liturgy without anyone else in the church seeming to notice her, without a greeting or even a glance.

Because God created us in his image and likeness, however, we have been created for love and relationship. We were created to have and to maintain a relationship with God, with others, and with the whole of creation. In fact, Adam and Eve lived this way until they lost their orientation toward God by grasping for the illusory promise of autonomy, of becoming like God. In this sense, health *is* a real and true relationship. Illness is the interruption of that relationship, the essential dialogue with God, with one's brothers and sisters, with oneself, and with creation. The Church is the "hospital" where we can rediscover the essential communion that our first parents lost, for the center of the Christian community is God, and health flourishes when we become truly what God has meant us to be.

What Lies within Us

God became human in Christ to show us what it really means to be human, that is, to share in God's life. The one who denies his or her relationship with God is like a story that is half-finished or a building that has been abandoned before completion. When the Risen Christ restores God's image in us, we are once more in communion with God through the Holy Spirit and participate in the kingdom. Maximus the Confessor (580–649) wrote that we, by the grace of God, can become that which God is. The Fathers of the Church called this transfiguration and transformation *theosis*. We are given the power to get up and walk out of a crippled past into a life of new meaning, joined to others in community, in peace with God, with ourselves, and with all of creation.

What does this say to those suffering from depression? To those struggling with emotional and psychological pain, *theosis* tells us that we are sons and daughters of God who share in God's glory, partake of God's nature, and are destined to inherit God's eternal kingdom. Scripture also tells us that we will inherit the kingdom (cf. Gal 4:4–6). Inheritance implies ownership. We won't just slip in the back door—the kingdom will belong to us as much as it belongs to our "co-heir," Jesus Christ (cf. Rm 8:17). In this spiritual hospital that is the community of believers, we learn that in all the sorrows and pain of depression, we are "more than conquerors through God who has loved us" (cf. Rm 8:37).

At the root of our "cure" is a personal act of faith in the love of God. No matter how hard the struggle is, we can hang in there in the spirit of Saint Paul who stated his faith in these words, "I consider that the sufferings of this present time are not worth comparing with the glory about to be revealed in us" (Rm 8:18).

Suggestion for prayer

Depression brings with it darkness and chaos. But God is present within as light, peace, and love. God is stronger than all the pain. The darkness is passing, the light is forever. The darkness comes only from wounds for which we ourselves are often not responsible. The light defines us as God's sons and daughters. Try praying the following:

You, Lord, are present in me as light. Nothing can take the light from me. You have chosen me to be your child. You hold me tight. Nothing can take me from you. The darkness and chaos will come and go as I am healed. But you, O Lord, will remain, because I am forever yours.

Write this prayer out for yourself and keep it with you so that you can pray it often.

———————

For one who is depressed

Write in a small notebook the names of the doctors and/or therapists you have seen, tests you remember having had, medications you have taken (as well as any major reactions or side effects that you remember), and your present medications with their dosages. Keep the notebook in a place where you will remember it. If you haven't had a complete medical check-up in a while, or you have changed doctors or therapists frequently and your present doctor doesn't have a complete history, bring this to her or his attention.

Do you have an acquaintance in your parish or someone you know who goes to the same Mass as you? A parish can be a source of stability and support, even if it is only through one or two people that you meet each Sunday at Mass. If you don't have any contacts in your parish, start by greeting others before and after the Sunday liturgy, or at other parish functions you may attend.

For a friend

Has your friend taken the first necessary steps toward well-being listed in this chapter? If not, share this information with him or her.

———————

Internet resources for support

- ○ Depression and Bipolar Support Alliance
  www.dbsalliance.org
- ○ National Alliance for the Mentally Ill
  www.nami.org
- ○ Depressed Anonymous (a twelve step program)
  www.depressedanon.com
- ○ Anxiety Disorders Association of America
  www.adaa.org
- ○ Federation of Families for Children's Mental Health
  www.ffcmh.org
- ○ WebMD
  www.webmd.com

CHAPTER 6

"I Just Want to Feel Better"

"I ask God every day to take this away and make me happy again. I don't think God hears me. Maybe God is sick of me asking." *Gerard*

"I do a lot of my recovery work in prayer. I talk to God about what I feel now and about the trauma I experienced in the past. God listens to me. He gives me the courage and strength I need to get through the times I feel more depressed." *Fr. Joseph*

If you want to be happy again then you have to start doing something yourself. I had to learn over and over again that if I waited around for someone else to give me what I thought I needed then I would have to wait a long time. I believe in God. I trust in God. Nevertheless, I don't expect God to miraculously do for me what I need to do for myself. Not that I don't believe in miracles. I do. I have simply come to realize that God's idea of the miraculous is sometimes an ongoing process of a deeper connection with him. So I've learned not to shortchange myself by insisting on miracles *my* way.

If I could, I would rid myself of temporal lobe epilepsy and have a perfectly stable personality. *Just think of all the things I could do if I were free from these mood swings,* I say to myself. But if I consume my energy wishing for something beyond my control and use it as a test for God to prove he loves me, I set myself up for disappointment. Instead of answering my prayers exactly as I want, God looks into my heart and responds to the deeper desires that he sees there, desires God himself has put within me. Perhaps he sees that I am asking for a penny when he wants to give me a million dollars. When I would be content to do something that makes me feel reasonably good about myself, God knows that I actually desire so much more. And so he takes the liberty to give me what I don't even know to ask for.

How Miracles Happen

Though we can't perform or command miracles, miracles do happen—sometimes gradually. Often we discover them only when we look back over our lives. We can see the gentle hand of God, the merciful caress of divine love threaded through the experiences of each day. We often see how God's power was hidden even in the efforts we made to help ourselves.

John, a college professor for thirty-two years, is married and the father of five. A few years ago, he went through a six-month period of deep depression. "They were the worst six months of my life," he says. "I was ashamed and confused. I still keep it a secret. Because I've been in therapy ever since that time, full-blown depression has never returned." John believes that he had suffered from depression all of his life and never knew it.

Two years after he began therapy, John went to Medjugorje on a pilgrimage to pray for healing. "I thought I would come back healed. When I returned home, my doctor suggested we try another medication, which made all the difference. It took care of my insomnia, irritability, and self-pity. I've been on this medication ever since. My healing came, but in a form I didn't expect."

John believes he has been a better servant to his students because of his familiarity with depression. He has been able to help young people suffering from depression get the help they need, and he has been able to support their families. John has taught music, theater, German, and courses in education. The creativity that often comes with depression—and which allows John to express himself in so many different areas—has been a gift to him in his career. "A lot of depressed people achieve great things. I believe it is the illness of creative people. Many musicians, artists, and poets have suffered from depression. Actually, if the Lord had healed me at Medjugorje, it might have ruined other things."

Prayer keeps John from sinking too low. "Sometimes I can't pray. I just say, 'Jesus.' Somehow I know my prayers are heard." Prayer is also a bond between John and his wife. "My wife has been a huge support to me. We say simple prayers together every evening. In the morning, we pray the morning offering. Praying together relieves a lot of tension for my wife because it isn't easy living with someone who is mentally ill."

This story is similar in its own way to the legend of a bird in a forest full of animal friends. The bird was known for her swift flight, and thus she was called *She-who-flies-swiftly*. The magnificent coloring of her wings flashed in the sunlight as she soared in and out of the trees of the forest. One day She-who-flies-swiftly broke one of her wings. She fell to the forest floor, and dragged herself near a tree for safety. After a little while, the Lord of the forest found She-who-flies-swiftly. He gently picked up the frightened bird and passed his hands over her broken wing before putting her down. The other birds were delighted. They thought, certainly She-who-flies-swiftly would be darting about through the forest once more. But She-who-flies-swiftly still wasn't able to fly. Instead, she stayed beneath a tree, lifting up her sad voice to the sky. The mournful notes continued through the days and nights, becoming always stronger and stronger. The forest had never heard the beauty of her song before. In the night hours, the other forest animals would quiet down and listen to her music, which grew more and more beautiful. She-who-flies-swiftly had learned to sing out of the depths of her sorrow and her loss, and her music captivated the hearts of all who heard it. She-who-flies-swiftly never flew again, but the healing touch of the Lord of the forest had given her the gift of song and a new purpose in life.

Those with the courage to walk all the way through the journey of depression discover the new gifts they are given. That is why John could remark, "Looking back on my life, I wouldn't want to change anything."

Starting with the Basics

Getting out of bed

The little miracles God brings about in our lives include such basic things as the strength to get out of bed in the morning. Those suffering from depression know how hard this can be when any day, every day, all day is one black hole of the overwhelming effort just to live. They just want the struggle with depression to end. They don't want to wake up to the same thing day after day.

But healing starts in small ways. With the help of a therapist or friend, choose an appropriate time for rising. Make an agreement that this is the start of your day. Set the alarm clock next to you, along with a reminder that this is your agreement. Sometimes being responsible to someone you respect or who knows you is a helpful motivation. From the small things done daily you can build up to new habits that can facilitate your journey to healing.

Diet

A sense of well-being is often connected to the care we take of our bodies. What we eat affects how we feel. Fruits and vegetables have a better effect on moods than do junk foods high in fat, sugar, and salt. Sugar is the biggest culprit when it comes to mood altering substances. It can cause mood elevation, hyperactivity, fatigue, mood instability, depression, exaggerated moods, headaches, irritability, and distorted and exaggerated anxiety. Avoiding foods high in sugar can be the first step toward a diet that assists your growth to wholeness.

Another culprit is caffeine. For many, being more conscious of caffeine intake is a good start to lessening the intensity of mood swings. Because many depend on that first cup of coffee in the morning, or coffee breaks throughout the day, it may be difficult to monitor caffeine intake. It is helpful to find another beverage you enjoy as much (other than tea, cola, or hot chocolate, which are also high in caffeine) in order to gradually reduce the amount of caffeinated beverages consumed each day.

Some people have also found dairy products to be a contributing factor to their mood swings, as well as wheat products, eggs, meat, and tomatoes.

You may be asking yourself if there is anything left to eat that will promote mood stability. If you speak with your doctor and a nutritionist, they can help you make a plan for a healthy diet that will promote your well-being. Your doctor will also be able to inform you if weight gain/loss is a side effect of the medication you are taking. Together you can discuss diet modification and exercise to deal with any weight gain or loss.

Exercise

The value of exercise for physical and mental well-being is constantly before our eyes. It is almost impossible to flip through a magazine without encountering at least one ad for exercise equipment, gyms, or exercise classes. Even ads for medication use pictures of people cycling or walking to "advertise" a healthy lifestyle. We are a health-conscious generation, at least in theory.

Maybe you've looked at such ads and turned the page. If you are depressed, just seeing the trim, perfect bodies of the models in these ads can make you feel even worse about your own appearance. It seems much less threatening to stay at home and say you'll find a way to exercise on your own. *After all*, you tell yourself, *it just takes going for a walk. . . .* But somehow, that walk never happens. Or maybe it happens once. Good exercise habits may be difficult to start, especially if weight gain is a side effect of your medication. Nevertheless, exercise will make you feel better. The hardest step is actually beginning. Here are some ideas to help get you started:

- Choose a form of exercise you can enjoy, perhaps swimming, dancing, or yoga.
- If you choose to walk, find an exercise soundtrack or lively, upbeat music to walk with.
- Plan to walk through a park a few times a week with a fellow employee or friend.

○ Offer to help someone who gardens and commit yourself to it once or twice a week.

○ Join an exercise program or a gym if a membership will help you commit to exercise.

Light

Just being outdoors for a half hour each day is the most inexpensive way to avail yourself of the powerful effects of sunlight on your mood. When I go for a long walk after having worked indoors for several days, I quickly feel my spirits lifting. Today more and more research is being done regarding the power of sunlight for elevating mood.

The next best thing to soaking in light from the sun is to use full-spectrum lighting where you live and work. Full-spectrum lighting contains the same rainbow colors and the same amount of near ultraviolet light as sunlight. You can purchase full-spectrum lighting at a hardware store.

Some people seem to need more sunlight than others. Certain seasons of the year, with shorter and darker days, seem to bring down some people's moods and increase their depression. People who experience depression during these darker seasons may have seasonal affective disorder (SAD). Exposing yourself to sunlight or full-spectrum light during these times of the year may be an unexpected key to lifting your spirits.

The miracle of coming out of a depression or learning to live graciously with a persistent mood disorder takes a combination of physical, psychological, and spiritual insight.

Dream

Despite the inner pain, depression does have its "advantages" and there are people who would rather stay depressed in order to make use of them. I remember speaking with a chiropractor who had been instrumental in returning people to health, even after their doctor had said there was nothing else to do. However, one gentleman, when he started getting better, stopped treatment. He preferred to remain an invalid. This was an advantage to him, because reassuming the responsibilities of adult life was either too scary or too demanding for him. My depression and the problems caused by my stroke were serious enough to begin with, but they became a self-fulfilling prophecy over the years. My self-confidence had been so destroyed that the safety net of being "sick" was preferable to the unknown adventure of taking on new responsibilities and launching out into the unknown. If I spoke my mind, if I tried to motivate people, if I carried through on a project despite others' comments, I would have to leave the comfort zone of depression behind. I would no longer have a ready excuse for failure. I wouldn't have a cocoon to return to in order to nurse my wounds. I would expose myself to the evaluation of others instead of remaining safely out of reach where I could judge them. As you begin to heal, it can happen that a powerful struggle occurs between the "depressed" you and the you that strongly desires to move on.

When we have the possibility of stepping into the unknown, of risking failure, of beginning to live without the label "depression" written across our foreheads, we can unconsciously sabotage ourselves so that we remain in the safety net of being able to blame our failure on depression. After all, out of kindness and compassion for our situation, people probably don't expect much from us. Acting with responsibility in a new venture where our success or failure is determined solely by how well we handle ourselves can be very frightening. To accept the challenge of doing what we haven't done for months or years will draw attention. What if we fail? Well, it will prove that we are as human as the next person is. There are some tools, however, that can make the first steps less ominous.

○ First, get past mental blocks. Begin listing the names of the people in your life who have believed in you.

○ What people have been good role models in your life?

○ What have you appreciated most about them?

○ Before you became depressed, what was the one thing that ruined your chance of being successful at something you really wanted? What negative lesson did you learn? Is this lesson really true? Are you still letting it rule your life?

○ What about yourself now makes you the most proud?

○ What do you think God sees when he looks at you?

○ List the skills for which you are most grateful.

○ Name three things you'd really like to do.

○ If you could be anything, what three things would you be?

○ If you were to ask God for the one thing most important to you, what would it be?

○ What makes you most excited?

Next, take new steps—one at a time. Perhaps you feel something stirring inside: *I would like to apply for a new position. I wonder if I could teach that class. I would love to work on that project. I would be so happy if I could bring a sense of beauty to our home again.* After you settle on a goal, list for yourself the steps you think you should follow to achieve it.

Now rip up the list and begin to enumerate things you *wish* you could do in order to achieve your goal. What you *wish* will probably be more outlandish than what you *think* you can do, but that's okay. In this part of the exercise the sky is the limit.

Finally, list what you *really* feel like doing. What do you really see yourself doing? Find a place of prayer: a church, your room, a favorite place outdoors or in a park. One by one, present to God what you have written down: your dreams, your feelings, seemingly far-fetched impossibilities. Pay attention to your initial reaction to these ideas as you present them to God. Do you feel light, happy, excited, confident, and at peace? Or are there some ideas that leave you feeling negative, fearful, closed in on yourself, cut off from God or others? Over several weeks, bring these ideas to prayer, asking God to help you see his dream for you rooted in your heart. As you begin to cross out ideas that leave you with a dead feeling, begin to concentrate your attention on the ideas that leave you with a feeling of life and hope. Ask God to show you how you can best achieve your goal in a way that is good for you, that serves others, and that pleases him. When you and God have decided on a direction, ask him to bless it. As you begin taking steps toward your goal, pay attention to what you feel within your heart. You can repeat steps of this process as often as needed, asking God for direction and strength.

It is strange but true that we "get" something out of depression, even as it drains us of life. By unmasking our attempts at self-sabotage, we can walk into a future of hope with God's dream for us written in the depths of our hearts.

Suggestion for prayer

The Sign of the Cross is a prayer of blessing made by tracing with our right hand the figure of the cross on our forehead, our breast, and our shoulders while saying, "In the name of the Father, and of the Son, and of the Holy Spirit. Amen." The Sign of the Cross symbolizes God blessing us, God embracing us with blessings. We recall the death of Jesus on the cross, a death that was an outpouring of love for us. The Sign of the Cross is a reminder of this forever love, a love that abides in us forever. Make the Sign of the Cross often. As you make this simple gesture, let it remind you that you are blessed in mind and heart and all your being. Through this prayer, which you can pray any time in the day or night, let God bring calm, and peace, and comfort to you. "Come to me," God says through this prayer. "Do not be afraid. Before you take one step, I reach out to embrace you and bless you."

For one who is depressed

When a person is depressed, it is difficult to begin cultivating healthy habits. Choose two or three concrete suggestions from this chapter that you can begin to practice, even in a small way.

For a friend

Express to your friend that you know God has a dream for him or her and that it will be clear in time. Support your friend through any changes he or she has decided to make.

Strategies for raising your self-esteem

○ Celebrate your accomplishments.
○ Be content with less than perfection.

- Realize that you haven't been defeated; you're working through your problems.
- Accept that it may take longer to accomplish your goals.
- Take things in stride.
- Make sure that you talk with people who support you.
- Think of yourself as a good and positive person.
- Believe in yourself as a child of God.
- Pray to the Trinity within you.
- Believe others who affirm your worth.
- Know that mental illness is no cause for shame.
- Take practical steps—even small ones—toward the new goals you have for your life.
- Surround yourself with people who are "survivors." Enjoy good reading, beautiful music, celebration.
- Learn something new every day about the challenges that you face.
- Network with others as much as possible.
- Be determined to get more out of life.
- Realize that those who treat you poorly are saying more about themselves than about you.
- Live one day at a time.
- Do work that you feel good doing.
- Pursue hobbies and crafts.
- Use creative expression (draw, paint, write, dance, etc.).
- Take small risks in a safe place.
- Be around people you like and who like you.
- Write down all the things that are good about you.
- Educate others around you about mood disorders and self-esteem issues.

CHAPTER 7

"I Can't Stop Crying"

"The hardest thing I ask of myself is 'Why me?'" *Juan*

〜

"God has a dream for me and somehow, somewhere, this is all part of that dream. I learned to stop fighting and instead listen to God's voice calling me. In hindsight this experience of depression has led me to be able to slowly become the 'compassion of Christ' for others." *Ralph*

Once a man received a letter from a business executive that stated he wanted to hand over to him a large sum of money. The gentleman didn't say where the money had come from or upon what conditions the money would be given. He only said to expect him within a year.

Now the surprised recipient of this good news took a long look around his house and thought about his job and friends. Obviously, he would have to make some changes before the money-bearing guest arrived. His front lawn would need a face-lift, the interior of his house needed a fresh coat of paint, and new entertainment equipment should be purchased somehow. He then began to consider that neither his friends nor his position at the company where he worked would make a favorable impression. Perhaps he had better begin moving in better circles and putting in more hours at his job.

He made a list of what he needed to do before his guest would arrive. He began working on improving his yard, home, and self, while running up bills on his credit card and promising payment for services. He worked extra hours with the hope of gaining a promotion, and for six months barely had time to catch a few hours of sleep before he was up and running again.

Then the long-awaited writer of the letter came to town on a business trip. In between appointments, he called at the man's house several times, but only met the painter or landscaper, who were never sure exactly when the owner of the house would be back. One day, the business executive drove up just as the owner of the house was leaving without so much as a backward glance. So the business executive left a note that read, *May I meet with you? A friend.* And he left a phone number. When the owner returned home, he found the note, but crumpled it up in his hand and tossed it into the garbage. *I don't have time for this,* he thought.

The next morning he opened his front door and, in his hurry to get to work, he almost ran over his would-be benefactor. "My friend," the well-dressed gentleman said gently, "I was hoping to speak with you."

"I don't know you," replied the irritated owner, walking past hurriedly.

"I know you don't, but may I come over to see you one evening?"

"Look, I'm really very busy; I haven't a free evening for the next two weeks. And I really have to run now."

"As you wish," the gentleman said. "But I really would like to meet with you before I leave town."

"Well, leave your number and I'll see about it."

The executive did as he was asked and went away. At the end of three weeks, his business completed, he reluctantly left town. Upon arriving home he sent a letter to the owner of the house explaining how he had tried to deliver the money, but couldn't since the man seemed to have no time.

When the man received the letter and realized his mistake, he wrote back quickly, "I was busy preparing for your arrival. I wanted to fix things up to be able to welcome you in the way you deserve."

One week later, an envelope appeared in the mailbox. Trembling, he opened the envelope to find three handwritten lines on a single sheet of paper. "You didn't need to do anything for me. I knew all about you. The money was my *gift* to you."

God is the friend who wants to meet you with a gift. God doesn't need to see in you a perfectly balanced personality before considering you worthy of his gifts. God knows you just as you are, with your history, your fears, your needs, and tears that perhaps never seem to stop falling. God loves you just as you are. God is the one who loves you most, with your garbage, limitations, and problems, as well as the beauty that you may not be able to see at this time. Nothing in your life could make you any less beautiful in God's eyes. Do not make the mistake of thinking you need to impress God. God is walking toward you always, arms outstretched, able to help you find meaning in everything. What is most needed is that you allow God to impress *you*. Let God impress you with his love. Even if you feel nothing when you read about God's love for you, keep believing. One day you will no longer need to believe because you will know. I have experienced this myself, and I have seen it in others.

Is Your God Good?

God's love can remain very abstract. We want, instead, to touch that love, to know it, to be embraced by it, to feel it concretely, to experience it as true. It is possible to know God's love in this way. Often, if God's love is to *be real,* people who are suffering from depression will need to build a bridge for themselves between the experience of God's love and the personal experience of being loved by another person. Building on the positive images of actually being loved by someone enables you to experience tangibly God's love for you and to involve your whole person in that experience. Believe that God is at least as loving toward you as some other person who has acknowledged, accepted, or affirmed you. If God isn't as loving as the best people you know, then you do not yet know God. Through Scripture, God reveals the characteristics of his immense love.

God reveals himself to us as "tender, compassionate, and constant."

The LORD passed before him, and proclaimed,
"The LORD, the LORD,
a God merciful and gracious,
slow to anger,
and abounding in steadfast love and faithfulness,
keeping steadfast love for the thousandth generation"
(Ex 34:6–7).

God's love is expressed as a safe love. God is one on whom we can depend.

When Israel was a child, I loved him,
    and out of Egypt I called my son.
The more I called them,
    the more they went from me;

they kept sacrificing to the Baals,
  and offering incense to idols.

Yet it was I who taught Ephraim to walk,
  I took them up in my arms;
  but they did not know that I healed them.
I led them with cords of human kindness,
  with bands of love.
I was to them like those
  who lift infants to their cheeks.
  I bent down to them and fed them (Hos 11:1–4).

God acknowledges our essential dignity, a dignity that psychological problems cannot touch or diminish.

But now thus says the LORD,
  he who created you, O Jacob,
  he who formed you, O Israel:
Do not fear, for I have redeemed you;
  I have called you by name, you are mine.
When you pass through the waters, I will be with you;
  and through the rivers, they shall not
   overwhelm you;
when you walk through fire you shall not be burned,
  and the flame shall not consume you.
For I am the LORD your God,
  the Holy One of Israel, your Savior.
I give Egypt as your ransom,
  Ethiopia and Seba in exchange for you.
Because you are precious in my sight,
  and honored, and I love you,
I give people in return for you,
  nations in exchange for your life.
Do not fear, for I am with you;

I will bring your offspring from the east,
    and from the west I will gather you (Is 43:1–5).

God appreciates us. He finds his delight in those whom he has created.

The nations shall see your vindication,
    and all the kings your glory;
and you shall be called by a new name
    that the mouth of the LORD will give.
You shall be a crown of beauty in the hand of the LORD,
    and a royal diadem in the hand of your God.
You shall no more be termed Forsaken,
    and your land shall no more be termed Desolate;
but you shall be called My Delight Is in Her,
    and your land Married;
for the LORD delights in you,
    and your land shall be married.
For as a young man marries a young woman,
    so shall your builder marry you,
and as the bridegroom rejoices over the bride,
    so shall your God rejoice over you (Is 62:2–5).

God is concerned for our welfare.

For surely I know the plans I have for you, says the LORD, plans for your welfare and not for harm, to give you a future with hope (Jer 29:11).

Stake Your Life on God's Love

Saint Edith Stein, also known as Saint Teresa Benedicta of the Cross, was born into a Jewish family on October 12, 1891. A philosopher who became a Catholic on January 1, 1922, Edith entered a cloistered Carmelite convent and died at Auschwitz.

A brilliant student, Edith graduated with the highest honors in 1916, and the well-known philosopher and phenomenologist, Edmund Husserl, chose her to be his research and teaching assistant. Her joy at her own success, however, was marred. All around her there raged World War I, with its hundreds of thousands of casualties, causing Edith unspeakable suffering. Among the war's victims was a dear friend, Adolf Reinach, who had first introduced her to Husserl. Though Edith traveled to be with and console Reinach's widow, she found herself consoled by his widow instead.

Edith continued to study, translate, teach, and lecture until 1933, when Hitler's regime and laws stripped non-Aryans of all their rights and dismissed them from all professional employment. On April 19, 1933, Edith's work as a lecturer at the Catholic Pedagogical Institute of Münster was terminated. She could not ignore the ominous signs of the coming suffering of the Jews in Germany and the hopelessness of her countrymen. A growing sense of foreboding gradually led to a deep despair. She said once that she couldn't even cross the street without hoping that she would be run over and it all would be ended.

During a Eucharistic holy hour at the Carmel of Cologne, shortly before she joined the community, Edith prayed, conscious of the shadow that hung over her beloved Germany. As she continued to pray for her people, she felt that it was the cross of Christ that was being laid on the Jewish people and that she desired to accept it willingly. She desired to carry the cross, though she did not know how. As the holy hour ended Edith felt that she had been heard, that somehow in the future she would indeed bear the cross with Christ.

When Edith entered the Carmel of Cologne and later received her new name, Sr. Teresa Benedicta of the Cross, she alluded to this night of prayer. It was the name she requested and she received it exactly as she had requested. In the Carmel she learned more of what it meant to be wedded to the Lord in the sign of the cross. She still bore within her the certainty that in some way she would take part in the destiny of the Jews which already was beginning to become clear, a destiny which for her meant more than losing a career and the holocaust of her people. In this destiny she recognized the cross of Christ and she desired to take it upon herself in the name of all.

Edith Stein's last philosophical work, completed in the monastery for the fourth centenary of the birth of John of the Cross, is entitled *The Science of the Cross*. On August 2, 1942, Edith and her sister Rosa Stein were arrested for being Jews. Her superior tried to shield the two sisters, but she could not save them. After they were arrested, she went to Sr. Teresa Benedicta's room and found the completed manuscript of *The Science of the Cross* lying open, the last sentences having been finished that very day.

Some time later the prioress of the monastery received a letter from Sr. Benedicta dated August 5, 1942, which read, "I am happy about everything. One can gain a science of the cross only if one feels the weight of the cross pressing down with all its force."[1]

On the evening of August 7, 1942, the Stein sisters boarded a train destined for Auschwitz. Together with other religious of Jewish heritage, they died in a gas chamber at Auschwitz on August 9, their bodies thrown into a ditch.

Edith Stein left these words, "I believe in God. I believe that the nature of God is love, I believe that man exists in love, is upheld by God, is saved by God."[2] Edith Stein says to those who are depressed: *Stake your life on God's love. Believe in the mystery of the cross.* Even if you are angry with God, believing God has "given you" this illness or these problems, still stake your life on God. Stake your life on the waters of Baptism that wash your soul. Stake your life on your true dignity as a son or daughter of God. Stake your life on the only One who can keep you safe.

Suggestion for prayer

Obtain some holy water from your church to keep in your home. Blessed water reminds us of cleansing and healing. Water is used to clean and to heal. The Church encourages Catholics to bless themselves with holy water when they are in danger from storms, sickness, tragedy, or other calamities. Holy water can be stored in a clean jar or you can purchase a small holy water font that you can hang up in your room. When I was growing up we always had holy water in each of our rooms. Blessing ourselves with holy water was the first thing we did in the morning and the last thing we did at night. You can pray a short prayer as you bless yourself with holy water, such as, "By this holy water and by your Precious Blood, bring me peace of mind and heart, O Lord."

For one who is depressed

Keep a small notebook by your bed. Each evening write down the names of one or two people who have shown you a glimpse of God's care and concern for you.

For a friend

In a moment of prayer, look over the past few times you have been with your friend who is suffering from depression. Are you happy with the way you have shown care and concern for him or her? Is there something you would like to change? Talk to Jesus about it.

―――――⟫●⟪―――――

Types of depression

Depressive disorders come in different forms. There are several diagnoses for depression, determined mostly by the intensity and duration of the symptoms and their specific cause, if that is known. Depression is a treatable illness. The unique form that it takes in each person means that the treatment will be tailored to each individual.

Major depressive disorder: a combination of symptoms that interfere with a person's ability to work, sleep, eat, study, and find pleasure in activities that once brought that person joy. Major depression can prevent a person from functioning normally, disabling a person to the point where they are unable to work. Some people have only one episode of major depression, but others have multiple episodes.

Dysthymic disorder or dysthymia: a long-term experience (over two years) of symptoms of depression that is not severe enough to disable a person, but is sufficient to prevent normal functioning or feeling well.

Minor depression: the experience of symptoms of depression for two weeks or longer that do not meet the criteria for major depression.

Bipolar disorder: characterized by cycling mood changes— from extreme highs (e.g., mania) to extreme lows (e.g., depression). Also called manic-depressive illness.

Cyclothymia: a milder form of manic depression. Mild forms of mania alternate with mild bouts of depression. The symptoms are much less severe than full-blown bipolar illness. Instability in professional and personal relationships due to unpredictable moods and irritability make those who suffer with cyclothymia difficult to live with and depend on. The cycles of cyclothymia are far shorter than in manic-depression and cyclothymics often do not seek treatment. They are extremely productive when they are in their hypomanic mode.

Some forms of depression develop under unique circumstances:

Psychotic depression: a form of depression that occurs when a person has major depression plus a form of psychosis such as a break with reality (delusions) or hallucinations.

Postpartum depression: a form of depression that is much more serious than the normal feelings women have after giving birth, when hormonal and physical changes combined with the new responsibilities for caring for a child can be overwhelming. Post-partum depression usually appears six to eight weeks after giving birth. Postpartum depression is a treatable illness.

Seasonal affective disorder (SAD): a form of depression that occurs during the winter months, when there is less natural sunlight. The depression generally lifts during spring and summer. Researchers have also uncovered a form of summer depression triggered by severe heat or intense light. This form of depressions occurs from June to August, but may be part of other depressive disorders as well.

Existential depression: brought on by a crisis of meaning or purpose. Transitions, a change of role at work, and a renewed sense or questioning of the larger meaning of life may trigger an existential depression. A number of researchers believe that a person's depression often has a connection to a lack of success in finding his or her passion in life, a connection to their deep inner wellspring of life.

Depression, not otherwise specific: This diagnosis is made when a person has a serious depression, but not severe enough for a diagnosis of major depression and who is not depressed long enough for a diagnosis of Dysthymic disorder, which requires depressive symptoms to have lasted two years. It includes those who continue to be depressed in response to some traumatic event.

Adjustment Disorder, with depressed mood: a form of mild to moderate depression following a stressful event where the resolving of the problem created by the stressful event receives the emphasis. Many times when there doesn't appear to be a solution to a problem following a psychosocial stress, a person can become depressed.

CHAPTER 8

"I'm Going Crazy!"

"There are so many voices in my head. Lord, which one is yours?" *Sean*

✑

"I found that when I am having obsessive thoughts of guilt pounding in my head I frequently repeat, 'Jesus, I trust in you' and seek counsel especially through the sacrament of Reconciliation. Jesus's mercy is far greater than anything I can do. I also find turning to Mary with the Hail Mary or the *Memorare* has brought peace to my mind and heart many, many times." *Linda Rose*

When someone says, "I'm going crazy!" the emphasis is nearly always on the last word: *crazy*. What does "crazy" feel like for you? For me crazy feels as if my mind's on overload and there are thunderstorms in my head. It is at these times that I become overwhelmed by little things and want to sit on the curb and cry. For each of us "crazy" feels a little different. Unfortunately, we too often pass over the subject of the sentence: "I." "*I* am going crazy!" This "I" is a very important word that denotes *ourselves*. Who is this *self*?

I Am the Home of the Trinity

At the outset of our pilgrimage on earth as Christians—whether it began when we were infants or later—we were washed in Baptism. These waters are the physical, visible expression of Christ who died on the cross and then was raised up from the grave. All Catholics were submerged into these baptismal waters and, at that moment, came into direct contact with Christ who has died and risen from the dead. At that moment we were infused with new life: Christ's life was poured into us.

When the person to be baptized is submerged under the water (or the water is poured on his or her forehead), that person dies and is buried with Christ. As the person rises from the water, he or she rises with Christ to new life. Often all we see, if we attend a Baptism ceremony, is a few drops of water poured on the baby's forehead, and we hear the words, "I baptize you in the name of the Father, and of the Son, and of the Holy Spirit." We may not be aware of what is truly happening. At the moment of Baptism, Christ's death and resurrection penetrate the one being baptized. The water and the words put the person into direct contact with the Lord. All of the salvific power of the death and resurrection of Christ is engraved within the person, because Jesus himself lives in him or her now. It is true. It is real.

Each day our Baptism brings us again to a radiant newness. Sin and evil can no longer dominate us, because within us is the One who conquers evil; the One who took all sin, all tears, all sickness, all evil upon himself. Baptism transforms the entire being of the person. You become nothing less than the home of the Holy Trinity, the temple of the Holy Trinity, inhabited by the Most High God. All of heaven is within you!

Christ is the Victorious One who in his death and resurrection conquered evil. Death, sin, unhappiness, and destruction cannot have the last word. The last word is the victory of Christ and his triumph and fullness. No longer is there death that cannot bring life, pain that cannot generate fullness, sadness that cannot convert into profound joy. There are no limitations, fragilities, psychological pain, or mood disorders stronger than the Resurrected One. We are children of the victory of the Resurrection. If only this truth burned within us!

If we have faith, if we keep loving and hoping through the tears, then the joy of the resurrection, the glory of the God who is with us, will transform our sorrow into a calm and radiant certainty of God's love. Though now we cannot see the ultimate victory—on this earth we still live in a vale of tears, and unhappiness is a part of our human reality—sadness will not remain the last word because we are with Someone who has already conquered death and pain. He has transformed all pain into victory. This is our faith. This is our truest certainty.

What Drives Us Crazy!

Distorted thought patterns are part of what make us think we are going crazy. People who experience depression can be plagued by obsessive, irrational thoughts. These intrusive, repetitive thoughts are unrealistic and anxiety provoking. Most of us have to deal with a certain amount of this distorted negative thinking, but those with mood disorders can find it particularly crippling.

Listed below are thirteen common distortions or faulty thought patterns, which are easily identified because they cause other painful emotions (such as worry and anxiety) and can be the cause of ongoing conflicts with other people.

All-or-nothing thinking: Suffering caused by the inability to see a continuum, the various shades of gray, or the options in every situation. Situations are either right or wrong, black or white. There is no in-between, no room for mistakes. Usually with this type of thinking we minimize the positive aspects of life until they completely disappear. *Example:* If something isn't perfect, it's worthless.

Overgeneralization: Reaching a broad, generalized conclusion based on one piece of evidence. We do this all the time when we stereotype. However, if we consider our generalizations to be reliable, we end up making conclusions that are most probably false. *Example:* A woman isn't invited to a friend's party and concludes that no one wants her as a friend.

Catastrophizing: The irrational belief that something is far worse than it actually is. *Example:* A salesperson hasn't made a sale in two days and is terrified she is going to lose her job.

Control fallacies: A thought pattern by which you believe you are in charge of the whole universe or everyone else is but you. Someone with control fallacies holds themselves responsible for everything that goes wrong. Either a person has total responsibility for things or feels they have no responsibility at all and takes on the role of a helpless victim. *Example:* *"I can't possibly leave the office on time. The place would fall apart without the work I do at night."*

Filtering: The only things that are seen or heard are those one chooses to notice. You unconsciously let in only the information that matches the way you feel about yourself. *Example:* A coach hears all the complaints, the rejection, and allegations of unfairness regarding his coaching and his team. However, he has blind spots that "filter out" any evidence of the worth of the team and compliments about their success.

Fallacies of fairness: The actions of others are judged according to preconceived ideas of what is fair, right, and just. *Example:* A mother says: *"If my children really cared about me, they'd come home for Christmas."*

Personalization: Everything is interpreted as a reflection on you and your self-worth. "It's all about me." Whenever there is mention of a problem, this person assumes he or she is being talked about. *Example: "The teacher said that not everyone is working hard enough to get an A. She must mean me."*

Self-blame: Assuming blame for everything, whether it's your fault or not. Even if things are out of your control, you blame yourself. *Example: "I'm afraid to ask my parents to come and visit because if they have an accident I'd never forgive myself."*

Emotional reasoning: Believing that everything we feel must be true automatically. *Example: "I feel ugly, therefore I am ugly."*

Demanding change: All hopes for happiness are placed in another person. We assume that if they are pressured enough they will change. *Example: "If only my wife understood me better, we wouldn't argue as much."*

"Should" statements: Seeing life and behavior through a set of indisputable rules about how everyone should act. *Example:* Parents should never get angry or argue.

Magnification and minimization: Discounting the good and magnifying the bad. *Example*: At a board meeting, the CFO delivers an impeccable presentation. Everyone congratulates him on the wonderful job, but he apologizes profusely for his failure to respond to the one question he couldn't answer.

Mind Reading: Basing assumptions and conclusions on what you imagine the other person is thinking. *Example: "The office manager passed my desk three times this morning. She must be checking up on me because she thinks I'm not doing my job."*

All of us have a steady diet of one or more of these distorted thought patterns. It is important to recognize your own negative thought patterns and the emotions that accompany them in order to substitute truthful thoughts that bring peace. For example, instead of thinking, "I am useless," which only makes you feel more depressed, you might learn to realize, "I am a hard worker when I feel well. At this moment I must be gentle with myself and trust in God's help." (See also, Getting a Grip on Obsessive, Unrealistic Thinking, further on in this chapter, page 113).

For now, however, consider two or three of the above distortions you recognize in your own thinking. In a quiet moment, sit down with Jesus. Talk to him about each of these distortions. Are they wreaking any havoc in your life, in your relationships, in your work? Do you have any new insights into what is happening in your life? Let Jesus speak about them from his perspective. Write down what he says. Write down one thing you would want to say to him in reply.

Did you notice that all of these thought distortions cause you to magnify the negative in your life? Actually, it has been said that we spend 90 percent of our time dwelling upon the negative in our lives, which, in reality, is only a fraction of our life experiences. We only spend 10 percent of our time celebrating the positive and beautiful, the achievements and surprises, and our fulfilled desires. Start to turn that ratio around by adding a special time of gratitude into your day. Determine a time every day as your "gratitude space." Make that time sacred so nothing else squeezes it out of your schedule. Spend your "gratitude time" thanking God for the good experiences, surprises, and beautiful things that happened during the day. Continue this practice and you will gradually find that your mind reflects fewer distortions and more reality.

Suggestion for prayer

These Stations of the Cross can be prayed when you feel yourself caught up in a negative distortion of your reality. The traditional fourteen stations can be replaced by other "stops" along the *Via Crucis*. The particular Stations below each include a reflection and prayer that highlight one of the cognitive distortions reviewed in this chapter. You can use this Way of the Cross as a time to unite the suffering you experience with the suffering of Jesus.

✠ First Station ✠

Jesus in the Garden of Gethsemane

Jesus, when situations seem either a complete success or a devastating failure, help me to find the mystery of the "in-between" where failures are successes and some successes are partly failures. You redeemed us and gained for us eternal life through what seemed your failure on the cross. Jesus, in my moments of agony, may I feel you near to me as a comfort and guide.

✠ Second Station ✠

Betrayed by Judas, Jesus Is Arrested

Jesus, when I feel let down by people I have trusted or don't understand what someone's words or actions mean, give me the courage to ask for clarification and explanation, instead of making generalized conclusions on just one piece of evidence. Teach me to respect the mystery of the other person whom I feel has hurt me, as you maintained your respect for Judas until the end. Jesus, when my moods start plummeting because of something another says or does, hold me in your arms.

✠ THIRD STATION ✠

Jesus Is Condemned by the Sanhedrin

Jesus, help me keep the big things big, but especially help me keep all the little things in my life little. When everything seems to be turning into a catastrophe, I want to remember you standing before the Sanhedrin with self-respect, trusting that your Father was going to take care of you. Jesus, when my world seems to be spinning out of control, remind me of our Father's care.

✠ FOURTH STATION ✠

Jesus Is Denied by Peter

Jesus, help me to realize there are things that are out of my control and that no matter how hard I try, I cannot make everything perfect. Help me to enter the mystery of powerlessness, that moment when your handpicked apostle denied that he even knew you and left you to die alone. Did you wonder why you had worked so hard to teach this man, who, in the end, denied you? Or did you hand the future of your kingdom over to God, since your death meant the giving up of all control? Jesus, when I think I am in control, gently pry open my hands and help me let go. Teach me to laugh and play again.

✠ FIFTH STATION ✠

Jesus Is Judged by Pilate

Jesus, stand beside me when I feel like others are judging me or putting me down. Did you feel embarrassed when you were condemned in front of all those people? I feel like that some-times. I interpret people's comments, even the way they look at me, as a condemnation or ridicule. Jesus, when I feel like every-one's looking at me, hide me in the shelter of your love.

✠ Sixth Station ✠

Jesus Is Scourged and Crowned with Thorns

Jesus, this was so unfair. What were you thinking while the soldiers scourged you and then made fun of you, crowning you with thorns and mocking you as a king? I'd be angry with them for making a fool of me. But you saw the larger picture; you knew that sometimes others will treat us unjustly. Jesus, when I don't think that others are treating me fairly, help me to remem-ber that neither were you treated fairly, that you walked this road ahead of me, that in the mystery of suffering I can unite my suffering to yours and share in the work of salvation with you.

✠ Seventh Station ✠

Jesus Bears the Cross

Jesus, when you started out through the crowded streets of Jerusalem toward Calvary, what did you feel about yourself? After all that had happened to you, were you wondering if maybe you had been wrong? Maybe if you had done things a different way, you wouldn't have been condemned to die as a criminal. Were you afraid as the people bustled around you, try-ing to stay clear of the soldiers? Sometimes I feel negative about myself. I carry my cross of depression and I think I'm no good, a failure, and ugly. Jesus, when I feel this way about myself, help me to remember that it isn't true. Help me to carry my cross beside you, to look into your eyes, which always look on me with love, and to see there who I truly am.

✠ Eighth Station ✠

Jesus Is Helped by Simon the Cyrenian to Carry the Cross

Jesus, did you hope that someone would help you carry the cross, or were you surprised that the Roman soldiers asked Simon to take your cross on his own shoulders? Many times, I expect or demand a Simon to appear, for someone to change their attitude and help me out a little. When my Simon doesn't appear, Lord, you be my Simon. Don't let me become bitter and blame everyone else for my problems. Jesus, let me see your face, and I shall be saved.

✠ Ninth Station ✠

Jesus Meets the Women of Jerusalem

Jesus, the women were so compassionate. What did they see in you? It would have been so easy for you to curse the entire human race for the treatment you received. But you didn't fall into the trap of labeling everyone because of some people's actions. You were still open to accept the kindnesses those women showed you. When I make broad judgments because of the actions of a few, send me someone like the women on the road to Calvary to remind me of the beauty of life and the ultimate reliability of love.

✠ Tenth Station ✠

Jesus Is Crucified

Jesus, if you wanted to, you could have had the last word. You could have justified yourself, proven to everyone around your cross that you really were God's Son. "Come down off your cross and we'll believe," they taunted. You could have done that. Jesus, I find it so hard not to have the last word, especially when

I *am* right. Jesus Truth, may I trust that the truth will always come out in the end. It is not justifying myself that matters, but being in right relationship with you, with myself, and with others that ultimately counts.

✠ ELEVENTH STATION ✠

Jesus Promises His Kingdom to the Good Thief

The good thief had a lot of nerve to trust you in those last moments before his death. You could have told him that he should never have broken the law in the first place. You could have "given him a sermon." But you didn't. You saw that life is about more than rules, though they have their place. Life is about reconciliation and acceptance and love that creates goodness around itself. When I use "should" statements with others, or myself, teach me the mystery of creative love that can promise eternal happiness to repentant criminals.

✠ TWELFTH STATION ✠

Jesus Speaks to His Mother and the Disciple

It must have been hard for Mary to stand beneath the cross. People who wanted to see you dead surrounded Mary. She saw the child she had cradled in her arms stretched beyond recognition on the arms of the cross. She heard you promising the good thief eternal happiness in your kingdom. She received the charge of caring for John as a son. Truly, beneath the cross all of us became her children. Mary was able to hold the beauty and the pain of those last hours of your life together, neither lashing out in anger nor discounting the good. Jesus, entrust me again to such a wonderful mother, that I might neither discount the good in and around me nor magnify the bad. Mary, be my sure hope.

✠ Thirteenth Station ✠
Jesus Dies on the Cross

Jesus, no one knew your final thoughts as you died. There are the traditional "seven last words" recorded in the Gospels, but I wonder what else you were thinking. Did you think of me? Sometimes I think I'm a mind reader and am suspicious of other people's attitudes toward me. But I never have to be afraid of what you think of me, because you can only love and create love all around you. Jesus, help me believe in your love.

✠ Fourteenth Station ✠
Jesus Is Buried in the Tomb

I can imagine all of nature in mourning when you, my Jesus, were buried in the tomb, as if all living things cradled your sacred, lifeless body. Jesus, I am never alone. I am cradled in your Father's arms, held by the universe, connected in the web of life and history with every other human person who has ever lived on this planet. And now I can feel how all creation groans and waits for my resurrection, for the moment of exaltation when tears will be no more and sorrow will be wiped away. Jesus, resurrected Lord and Savior, be my salvation. Amen.

For one who is depressed

Find a piece of music or art that helps you visualize and feel the presence of God within you. If it is a piece of art, put it in a prominent place where you will see it every day. If it is a particular piece of music, play it often, especially when you are down.

For a friend

Try to find a way to celebrate your friend as a temple of God. It could be as simple as being more supportive and respectful. Or you might want to send small Christian note cards or e-mail messages.

———————

Getting a grip on obsessive, unrealistic thinking

Those suffering with depression struggle with negative, irrational, obsessive thoughts. These thoughts not only make everything a "big deal" or a "catastrophe," they also may make it difficult to believe that God—or anyone else for that matter—loves you. They can make you question if life has any meaning or if you are alone and abandoned in the universe. Though these dark thoughts begin to lighten as the depression lifts, you can form a habit of "truthful" thinking by confronting such thoughts and by using mantras, which are repeated short prayers. Below are guidelines for changing these thoughts as well as some different mantras you could choose to pray. One may strike you as something you would wish to always say, or it could be helpful to alternate them on different days or according to your varying moods. The more you occupy your mind with thoughts that purify and strengthen, the less power depressive thoughts will have over you. Some of the mantras are traditional, some represent newer ways of approaching God, and finally some of them have been suggested to me and I have found them helpful in counteracting obsessive negative and "shaming" self-talk.

Basic guidelines for changing irrational thoughts

Statements, requests, expectations, and news can cause us a lot of stress and agony. The distress is created by how we deal with the incoming information or demands. Let's take two statements or demands from others that might spark irrational thoughts, which in turn, bring about emotional distress:

1. Someone says to you: You *should* do this or that.
2. Someone tells you about a specific event that will happen, which upsets you.

Evaluate the demand or the statement, e.g., 1. Do I really want to do this? Is it really in my best interest to do this? 2. It hasn't happened yet. What are the realistic probabilities that it will happen?

Take off the pressure, e.g., 1. I'm allowed to say no. If I say yes, there is no hurry and it won't be terrible if I find I have to change my mind. 2. If this happens it will be painful or frustrating, but it won't be terrible or catastrophic.

Make a plan, e.g., 1. Set small, realistic goals. Pace yourself. 2. Consider whether or not there is anything you can do to prevent the negative event from happening. If so, do it. If not, accept that you can't.

Mantras for finding peace and truth

- ○ Lord Jesus Christ, have mercy on me (the Jesus Prayer).
- ○ Jesus.
- ○ Spirit of Jesus, let me hear your gentle voice.
- ○ Lord, I am the apple of your eye.

❍ I have caught sight of you, my Love, and you are very beautiful.

❍ May it be done to me as you have said.

❍ In my heart, O Lord, I treasure your promises.

❍ I believe that God is love.

CHAPTER 9

"God, Where Are You?"

"One of the most difficult sufferings I've experienced from depression is getting through times of prayer. It can be nearly impossible to sit silently focused for any length of time without a gnawing anxiety growing inside me or the invasion of unpleasant memories or thoughts. At such times I find it useful to practice the prayer of presence, staying at prayer only as long as I can remain so peacefully. Quietly I am aware of God's presence inside me, around me, with me. I am present to God. I love God and I know God loves me. This prayer doesn't demand anything else. No great thoughts or over-whelming emotions are necessary." *MaryJo*

Saint John Vianney, the famous curé of the tiny French village of Ars, is most popularly known as the holy and humble priest who spent sixteen to eighteen hours a day hearing confessions. Long processions of people came to this out-of-the-way village to seek his advice. He practiced extraordinary penances and fasts for the conversion of sinners and was subject to diabolic persecution all his priestly life. It is said that the devil revealed once that if there were but three priests in the world like the Curé of Ars, the devil would lose his kingdom.

What is less known is the overwhelming depression that weighed on John Vianney's soul throughout his life. Though he was the most sought after man in all of France, he seemed incapable of seeing the immense amount of good he was doing. Despite the tens of thousands of pilgrims who traveled to Ars each year in the hope of receiving the sacraments or a word of advice from him, he believed himself useless. The priest who had reawakened the faith of a village and set all of France aflame through his preaching and holiness, felt God so far from him that he was afraid he had no more faith. He believed himself to have no intelligence or gift of discernment. It is as if there was a veil over his eyes so that he could see nothing of what God was doing for others through him. The Curé feared he was ruining everything and had become an obstacle in God's way.

The root of John Vianney's severe depression was his fear of doing badly at every turn, and the thousands who traveled to Ars increased his terror. It never occurred to him that he might have a special grace. Instead, he feared that the long line of penitents to his village church was a sign that he was a hypocrite. He feared facing the judgment with the responsibility for all these people on his conscience. There was not a moment when he felt that God was satisfied with him. A great and profound sadness possessed his soul so powerfully that he eventually could not even imagine relief.

Whenever the tempests of depression seemed powerful enough to drown him in the vision of his own miseries, the Curé would bow his head and throw himself before God like "a dog at the feet of his master." In this way he would allow the storm to pass without changing his resolve to love and serve God if he could. Yet he kept this pain so private that, except for a few confidants, most people saw only tranquility and gentleness in his bearing.

Jesus Is in the Darkness with You

You may discover that the shadows and tempests of depression alter the way you look at God and the way you believe God looks at you. When you pray you may be unable to sit still or to keep your mind focused for more than a few moments. Everything may appear to be a huge gaping hole of silence, all so useless. God may seem to be mocking your attempts to pray. I know people who have gone three, five, ten years without "praying," though they were faithful to setting time aside for prayer regardless of its seeming uselessness. In the haunting darkness where all communication had gone silent, they found loneliness, boredom, frustration, anger. Were they praying? Yes.

God's abiding love is deep within, never forsaking you in darkness. You are alone in the void with the Son of God—both of you keeping silent. Suffering with you is Jesus, the abandoned Son on the cross. When it is impossible to hold on to a thought or to pray, Jesus is praying and contemplating within the one who is suffering from depression. Day by day, moment by moment, groping in the darkness, you are not alone. Jesus is struggling with you. He is there feeling it all. Nothing goes unnoticed by him or his Father. Through Jesus's spirit who is in you, you can hope for peace.

Ideas for Praying When Depressed

Prayer for those suffering with depressive illnesses can be difficult or impossible. Those who feel let down by God or believe he has forgotten them or is punishing them will find it hard to follow the traditional methods of prayer. Anger and disillusionment can lead to a crisis of faith. In these cases it is helpful to look at prayer with a larger lense that includes art, music, walking, imagination, and nature.

If this is happening to you, try these forms of prayer and contemplative love:

1. *Draw a picture that represents your feelings or illustrate what is in your heart.*

2. *Try to find a quiet place.* Put on some soothing music. Take a few deep breaths, holding each one for a few seconds and then slowly exhaling. Relax. Feel the chair you're sitting on, your feet on the floor. Smell the scents in the room. Imagine Jesus coming toward you with a smile on his face. If you can, tell him how you are feeling right now: anxious, uncomfortable, fidgety, distracted, at peace, resigned, expectant. Tell him what things are like for you today. Open your heart to him. Feel his presence very close to you. Let his love into your heart. Thank him for this gift.

3. *Go for a walk.* Take some pleasant music with you. As you go, notice the sky, feel the season. Recognize what is around you. Feel at home right now. Offer your heart to God, even if your pain is deep. Though you may be alone on your walk, God is in your heart. Tell him what you see—the beauty around you. Tell him how you feel—even if it is dark. Remember he wants you to tell him everything in your life—joys and pains.

4. *Call to mind someone else you know who is hurting or sick.* Focus for a few minutes on what that person may be feeling and on what you would like to say to him or her. Lift this person up by name and ask a blessing on them.

5. *Hold a crucifix in your hands.* Close your eyes and imagine of Jesus in agony. Join your sufferings to his.

6. *If you're feeling low, go to a quiet place and hold your Bible.* Read Psalm 130 or focus on a phrase of it. Know that God is loving you through these moments of darkness.

7. *When you are unable to focus because your mind is racing, try to remember and to pray the words, "My God, I love you."*

8. *Turn on soft music.* Read this Bible verse over and over while thinking about it: "My God, my God, why have you forsaken me?" (cf. Mk 15:34). This is Jesus's own prayer of emptiness and abandonment.

9. *When you pass by your local church, stop in for a few minutes and sit in the quiet stillness. If possible, go to a church that has Eucharistic adoration and spend some time in adoration of Jesus present in the Sacred Host.*

10. *If you can't get up, lie still and repeat the name of Jesus over, and over, and over.* His love catches these words and he embraces you with love.

Where God Is

Sr. Thomas Halpin was diagnosed with bipolar disorder when she was thirty-eight. In one way, it was a relief for her to have an explanation for her psychotic episodes and suicidal thoughts. In another way, she felt that her life had come apart. Since she had often spoken with me, I was privileged to know some of her story. When I asked her how she kept praying through those years she said quite honestly, "I didn't think I was praying, but I had made a commitment to pray. I was convinced that Jesus was present in the Eucharist. I felt like I 'owed him time.' So I would just go to church and sit. Sometimes I even deliberately ignored God. I was so angry. Before my illness, I had been able to accomplish so much, and here I was, reduced to nothing. I thought God had played a dirty trick on me. It was this way for six or seven years.

"I complained on and on about what God had done to me, through session after session with my therapist. Finally, he said to me, 'Go home and think of all the things you have to be grateful for.' I left his office very angry. Who was he to tell me that? Later when I went to chapel, I stared at the tabernacle and started thinking. I saw faces. I saw my therapist. I saw my sisters. And I heard, 'This is where I am. You've been missing me, and I've been here the whole time. You won't find me in a vision or a miracle, because this is how I choose to work—through others and only through others.' That reflection made me realize more and more the personal investment God has in me and I have in him. It's been a long time since those days. I can talk to God easily. And now, I'm able to talk about love.'"

Sr. Thomas was faithful to a contemplative silence. Almost imperceptibly through the years something seemed to change, beautifully, as the dark sky changes during a sunrise. Sr. Thomas now has a strength, a depth, a compassion, a heart, a kind of prayer found in few people. She experienced a mystery in the life of Christ that many people never will. She had suffered Jesus's passion to the bitter end, and she had been resurrected more gloriously.

Suggestion for prayer

Create a prayer corner or a quiet place in your home. Put in it strong visual reminders of God, Mary, or a favorite saint: a crucifix, icon, picture, or statue. Keep one or two CDs of instrumental, praise and worship, or other favorite music handy to help set the mood or create an atmosphere in which you can sense God's presence and allow God to minister to you in your need. Incense sticks or small candles are strong sensory elements that can also help arrest depressive thoughts. When we cannot pray with words, simply watching a candle flame dancing in the darkness can help us enter into a contemplative peace. As you find motivational quotes, write them out and keep them in your prayer corner. Place there whatever else helps you lift up your mind and heart, and find peace and hope in prayer. God does not demand things of you in your prayer. God wants to give you so many gifts when you open your heart to him. Use whatever helps you open up in trust.

―――――――

For one who is depressed

Try to reflect on what it is like for you to pray. How would you like God to be there for you? Share this with God.

For a friend

Read a biography, an autobiography, or the writings of someone who has suffered depression or manic-depression. Some suggestions are: *An Unquiet Mind: A Memoir of Moods and Madness,* or *Touched With Fire: Manic-Depressive Illness and the Artistic Temperament,* both by Kay Redfield Jamison; *The Depression Workbook Second Edition: A Guide for Living with Depression and Manic Depression* by M. E. Copeland, et. al.; *Depression Fallout: The Impact of Depression on Couples and What You Can Do to Preserve the Bond* by Anne Sheffield; *The Noonday Demon: An Atlas of Depression* by Andrew Solomon; *A Brilliant Madness: Living with Manic-Depressive Illness* by Patty Duke, et. al.

―――――――

Healing Scriptures

The Scriptures contain the words God speaks to us. Find those passages that speak to you of God's love in a particularly strong way. Repeat these words often. Personalize them with your name, for they are truly addressed to you.

_____, "You are precious in my sight" (Is 43:4).

_____, "I am the light of the world, you are the light of the world" (Jn 8:12; Mt 5:14).

_____, "I have called you by name, you are mine" (Is 43:1).

_____, "Your grief will turn to joy" (Jn 16:20).

_____, "The Lord your God is your light" (Rev 22:5).

_____, "Live on in me, as I do in you" (Jn 15:4).

_____, "Cast all your cares on God, who cares for you" (1 Pt 5:7).

CHAPTER 10

"Don't Look the Other Way"

"Before, I used to go out and have a great time with my friends. Now they never invite me anywhere. I don't think they know what to say to me." *Caitlyn*

"One day a co-worker scolded me, 'You have taken long enough to work through whatever you need to work through. Get over it!' I was shocked, but I had the courage to stand up for myself and respond, 'Have I changed?' 'Well, yes,' she responded. 'Okay, then.' Everything has its own rhythm and healing does too. There is no timetable to keep, no right or wrong amount of time needed for healing." *Jeanine*

There is one thing worse than suffering depression and that is suffering depression alone. There are many reasons why we might shy away from people who are suffering depression. We may honestly not know what to say. Our attempts to solve another's problem may be met with frustration and defensiveness on the part of the person suffering with depression. Not knowing what to do to help can make us feel awkward and helpless. In frustration, we may decide that if the person suffering depression isn't going to get on with life, they'll just have to go on by themselves. Gradually, without really intending it, the depressed person is marginalized and soon forgotten.

Maintaining a concerned friendship with someone suffering with depression requires that we face the fact that we can't fix the situation any more than he or she can. Both sides have to learn the lesson of God's divine love. God came to companion us in our suffering by coming into our midst. In Christ, God learned what our suffering was like. God didn't tell us what to do to fix this suffering or show us how to sidestep it. He drew near to us. He suffered with and for us. He died in darkness, powerlessness, and abandonment to destroy the power of sin and evil, which held us captive, but he didn't take evil away and we still feel its consequences. God's divine love follows the dynamic of the cross.

When we draw near to someone who is suffering from depression, we too are drawn into this divine dynamic of compassion. The first thing we learn when we companion someone who is suffering with depression is that all survival, organizational, and problem-solving skills that work so well in other areas of our life have no place in this friendship. Only the dynamics of companioning, of being with, of suffering alongside another, as God has done for us in Christ, are operative here. Suffering makes both the one who is depressed as well as his or her friend feel very poor.

The poverty of depression offers another lesson of divine love. God revealed his glory in the broken body of his crucified Son. And still today, God's glory is revealed in vulnerability and brokenness. We sometimes erroneously think that God's glory is only apparent in magnificent cathedrals and great works of charity. But the cross—as God's choice for displaying his wisdom and power—shows us that God's glory is actually most evident in quiet, anguished suffering, such as the suffering a depressed person shares with his or her friend. The one who reaches out a hand in friendship begins to learn vulnerability and the poverty of powerlessness. But he or she will one day touch the presence of God in their friend.

Finally, a concerned person who consistently reaches out to a depressed friend comes to know the blessing of being trusted. Over time, both learn to rest in their poverty, discarding all pretenses. Both are able to give and receive. The paradoxical outcome of all this is that the friend discovers that he or she has received more than what he or she had given.

The Five Beatitudes of Companioning a Depressed Friend

Blessed are they who tear up labels.

When you have decided to begin or continue a friendship with someone who is suffering from depression, especially if he or she has been struggling with chronic or clinical depression for many years, it is easy to unconsciously assume a patronizing attitude: this "poor person" needs my help. If you think your friend is lucky to have you to help them, throw that idea out before you even start. Such a friendship will end in frustration and anger on both sides, because your friendship is with the person's illness, not with him or her as a person. You have already classified or "branded" your friend with a label. I am convinced that we hold many people hostage for their entire lives in cages made of labels. A label can destroy a person's future.

Likewise, in a Christian community there is no place for labels because there are no labels in the Gospels. In fact, Jesus scandalized the religious leaders of his day because he ate and drank with those who had been labeled "publicans and sinners" by the religious institution. Jesus's radical ideas of evangelical friendship were rooted in the heart of God "whose sun shines on the good and the bad" (cf. Mt 5:45), and "who loved the world so much that he sent his Son into the world to be its salvation" (cf. Jn 3:16). Jesus had no patience with labels, and neither should we.

To break open the cages in which you may subtly be locking yourself or a friend suffering from depression, it may be helpful to discover some famous people who have suffered or suffer from a mood disorder and yet have had a tremendous effect on the world.

Here are just a few:

Authors: Hans Christian Andersen, Arthur Benson, F. Scott Fitzgerald, Graham Greene, Ernest Hemingway, William James, Ralph Waldo Emerson, Herman Melville, Eugene O'Neill, Jean Stafford, Mary Shelley, Leo Tolstoy, Mary Wollstonecraft, Tennessee Williams, and Virginia Woolf.

Poets: Charles Baudelaire, William Blake, Lord Byron, Emily Dickinson, T. S. Eliot, Robert Fergusson, Thomas Gray, Gerard Manley Hopkins, Victor Hugo, John Keats, Mikhail Lermontov, James Russell Lowell, Edna St. Vincent Millay, Edgar Allan Poe, Ezra Pound, Anne Sexton, Delmore Schwartz, Lord Tennyson, Francis Thompson, and Walt Whitman.

Composers and Musicians: Samuel Barber, Ludwig van Beethoven, Anton Bruckner, Kurt Cobain, John Denver, Stephen Foster, George Frederic Handel, Gustav Holst, Charles Ives, Modest Mussorgsky, Robert Schumann, Peter Tchaikovsky, Hugo Wolf, and Bernd Alois Zimmerman.

Artists: Vincent van Gogh, George Innes, Ernst Ludwig Kirchner, Michelangelo, and Dante Gabriel Rossetti.

Statesmen: Menachem Begin (Prime Minister of Israel, Nobel Laureate), Winston Churchill, Calvin Coolidge, Abraham Lincoln, and Richard M. Nixon.

Saints: Saint John of the Cross, Saint Thérèse of Lisieux, Saint John Vianney, Saint Benedict Joseph Labré, and Saint Edith Stein.

People would be surprised to discover how many prominent and successful individuals today suffer from mood disorders. Among such individuals are: Roseanne Barr, actor, writer, comedienne (also has multiple personality disorder and obsessive compulsive disorder); Dick Cavett, writer, media personality; Tony Dow, actor, director; Kitty Dukakis, former first lady of Massachusetts; Patty Duke, actor, writer; Connie Francis, actor, musician; Peter Gabriel, musician; Charles Haley, athlete; Kristy McNichol, actor; Spike Mulligan, comic actor; Abigail Padgett, mystery writer; Murray Pezim, financier; Charley Pride, musician; Axl Rose, musician; William Styron, writer; James Taylor, musician; Robin Williams, actor, comedian.

It is unfortunate that we so often push aside those with depression, categorizing them as "useless," conveniently ignoring them, or patronizing them. We impoverish ourselves by not companioning and serving these great "poor ones."

Blessed are they who don't try to be a doctor.

One of the most important things a person suffering from depression needs is appropriate diagnosis and treatment. Encourage your friend to pursue professional medical care. A complete physical is essential for correct diagnosis. What looks like depression could be a symptom of an underlying organic problem. The person should make an appointment for an interview with a psychologist in order to determine their unique experience of depression. Is she suffering from generalized anxiety? Is he depressed because of a recent job loss? Is she exhibiting signs of post-traumatic stress, possibly indicative of traumatic events in her life?

Although you can't be your friend's doctor, you can encourage your friend to get professional help. You may need to encourage your friend to stay with the treatment until symptoms begin to abate, or to seek different treatment if no improvement occurs. Because each person's body chemistry is unique, the search for the medication or combination of medications that can help a person with depression can last over an extended period. It's essential to be persistent and patient. Encourage your friend to be hopeful and continue to try new medications as prescribed by his or her doctor until the right combination is found. Often when someone suffering from depression begins to pursue professional help, they immediately start to cut corners: "I don't really need to get all those tests"; "I think I know what the problem is, I don't need to go back to the doctor"; "I feel good now so I stopped taking my medicine." Cutting corners with depression always complicates the diagnostic process. Encourage them to stick with their treatment and to keep asking their doctor before making any major treatment decisions of their own.

You may be the only one with whom your friend shares what he or she is really feeling. This is an awesome trust. Welcome whatever he or she may wish to say to you without judging. Encourage your friend to share important information with his or her doctor.

Blessed are they who offer emotional support.

Depression can marginalize its sufferers so that they feel as if a door is quickly closing, shutting them off from the land of the living. But you can put your foot in the door to keep it open, even if just a crack. Call your friend. Send her e-mails or flowers. Invite him to go for walks, to the movies, or hiking. Invite your friend to go to church with you or to join with you in your parish activities. Take her along shopping, or ask him to accompany your family on a picnic. Pray with her over the phone. Send him e-mail promises of prayer and support. Offer diversion and company, but don't insist. Too many demands can increase feelings of failure.

Remember: your stable interest in your friend's welfare should not depend on any improvement on their part. Your fidelity lets her know she is accepted. Your support lets him know that you believe in him. Your friend can learn from you how to accept himself, to know that life is good, to believe that joy can eventually be experienced again.

Hans's sister Laura was extremely depressed. She had taken time off from work and stayed with her older sister because she was afraid to be alone. Hans lived on the other side of the country, but he made sure to call her once a week and write to her every two days. He remembers that he kept repeating to her that he loved her and Jesus loved her even more. Hans told her that he was praying for her and that he prayed that her guardian angel would protect her. Later, Hans said his sister told him that it was the thought of her guardian angel being with her that had been her greatest comfort.

This type of a friendship can be tested in two ways. What if the person never seeks professional help or, even with medication and therapy, still does not seem to improve? What if your friend becomes angry with you or accuses you of meddling in her affairs? Though you can encourage and be there for others, their decisions and journey are ultimately their own. God cares for them even more than you could ever care, and sometimes putting them in the hands of God is all—and actually the best thing—you can do. God has mysterious ways of saving each person. Your friend may never pursue wellness, and yet, in God's designs and their human weakness, they may be living an apostolate of suffering. The temptation to take control of your friend's situation may be great, but he or she needs to be free to seek wholeness in his or her own way. Such situations call for tremendous patience and freedom to both hold your friend and let him or her go their chosen way.

Blessed are the compassionate.

If someone were to ask you if you thought of yourself as a compassionate person, you might reply yes, or at least, "I believe so." However, the true meaning of the word compassion is more than mere sympathy or pity. It comes from the Latin root "to suffer with." To show compassion means sharing in the suffering "passion" of another. In his book, *Never Forget,* Henri Nouwen describes compassion as the capacity to enter into another's dark moments, into their pain, without running away. The great contribution Nouwen made to the caring profession was to call us to stay with people in the places in which they suffer without offering quick fixes, explanations, or promises. A lack of compassion often comes from the all too human rejection of suffering characteristic of our times. It is difficult to be truly compassionate.

Your journey of walking with someone in his or her pain begins with both compassionate and respectful silence. Here are some compassionate words that you might say:

○ "I love you."

○ "I care."

○ "You're not alone in this."

○ "I'm not going to leave you."

- "Do you want a hug?"
- "You are important to me."
- "We can ride this out together."
- "When all this is over, I'll still be here and so will you."
- "All I want to do now is give you a hug and a shoulder to cry on."
- "You're not crazy."
- "I can't imagine how hard this must be."
- "I'm sorry you're going through this."
- "I'm never going to say, 'I know how you feel' unless I truly do, but if I can do anything to help, I will."

Listed below are examples of uncompassionate words that should never be said to someone suffering with depression:

- "It's all in your mind."
- "I thought you were stronger than that."
- "Don't think about your problems. You should be grateful for what you have. There are other people who have nothing."
- "Happiness is a choice."
- "Well at least it's not that bad."
- "Get a grip."
- "There are other people worse off than you."
- "You are what you think."
- "The only one you're hurting is yourself."
- "Why don't you smile more?"
- "You're always worried about your problems."
- "Go have some fun for a change."

- ○ "I want the old you back. I don't like the way you are now."
- ○ "Maybe you need to trust God more."
- ○ "Just hang in there."
- ○ "You are your own worst enemy."
- ○ "My life isn't fun either."
- ○ "What's *your* problem?"
- ○ "Will you stop that constant whining?"
- ○ "Haven't you gotten tired of all this me-me-me stuff?"

Blessed are they who contemplate what God is doing.

Your friendship with someone who is depressed can become a new form of prayer. We spend most of our adult life analyzing and calculating. Neither of these, however, are building blocks of prayer. Prayer is about observing, contemplating, wondering, imagining. As you develop a friendship that leaves the other be, you may find the following suggestions helpful:

1. Remember occasions on which God has rescued you. Write them down. Offer gratitude to God for them. Contemplate what God has done in your own life.

2. Before meeting with your friend, spend some time in silence. Relax. Be calm and serene. Tell God that you want to contemplate what he will be doing while you and your friend are together.

3. Thank God in your heart every time you realize God has been helping your friend, even if your friend cannot see it. You will begin to see that God will help your friend in his own time. He has no timetable, no agenda. God is a

mystery. And so is your friend. Let God do the rescuing. You can count on God.

4. Pray for your friend.

5. Tell your friend you are praying for him or her. Occasionally point out what you see God doing in your friend's life. "It seems to me that God is letting you remember some beautiful times in your life when you felt loved by others." "You seem much more peaceful. God has given you a tremendous gift."

Suggestion for prayer

Sacred Scripture is full of passages that offer comfort and examples of how to companion those who are suffering in any way. Through the people in the story of salvation history, we see the same human emotions and struggles we face—and God's unchanging love for us and presence with us in every situation. Here are only a few of the many beautiful lines of Scripture for the friends of those with depression to contemplate.

"As the sun was setting, all those who had any who were sick with various kinds of diseases brought them to him; and he laid his hands on each of them and cured them" (Lk 4:40).

"Then some people came [to Jesus], bringing to him a paralyzed man, carried by four of them. And when they could not bring him to Jesus because of the crowd, they removed the roof above him; and after having dug through it, they let down the mat on which the paralytic lay . . . [Jesus] said to the paralytic, 'I say to you, stand up, take your mat and go to your home'" (Mk 2:3–4, 11).

"Come to me, all you that are weary and are carrying heavy burdens, and I will give you rest. Take my yoke upon you, and learn from me; for I am gentle and humble in heart, and you will find rest for your souls" (Mt 11:28).

"Jesus prayed, 'Father, if you are willing, remove this cup from me; yet, not my will but yours be done.' Then an angel from heaven appeared to him and gave him strength" (Lk 22:42–43).

"Mary stood weeping outside the tomb. As she wept, she bent over to look into the tomb; and she saw two angels in white, sitting where the body of Jesus had been lying. . . . They said to her, 'Woman, why are you weeping?' . . . She turned around and saw Jesus standing there. . . . Jesus said to her, 'Woman why are you weeping? Whom are you looking for?'" (Jn 20:11–13).

For one who is depressed

Trusting friends is difficult when one is depressed. It takes a lot of energy to interact with others. It is a great risk to believe and to hope that another will welcome and care about you when life itself seems to have given up on you. For one week, keep a small notebook in your pocket or purse. Jot down the times that you wish someone cared and would be there for you, as well as any behaviors or choices on your part that are keeping such a friendship from developing. For example, not joining others because you feel they won't want you around. This self-defeating behavior perpetuates a situation of isolation and loneliness. At the end of the week, decide on one thing you can change in your own life that would make it possible for deeper friendships to blossom. As you begin to make changes in your life, what surprises you?

For a friend

After you speak with a friend suffering from depression, take a moment to jot down the things that you remember having said. Try to notice if you expected your friend to be better or do better because of what you were saying to him or her, or if you just relaxed and tried to show her or him God's love.

Four tips if a friend or family member is depressed

First: Inform yourself. Read as much as you can about depression. There is ample information available from medical institutions on the Internet. Depression is a serious illness that requires professional attention. Depression isn't the result of a character flaw. It's not laziness. It's not simply a case of "the blues." People with depression aren't faking it and cannot "snap out of it."

Second: Express your concern by listening to your friend or family member if he or she wants to talk. Respect his or her desire for privacy if they would rather not talk. Asking how you can help lets your friend or family member know that you are willing to be supportive, even if he or she cannot suggest what you can do. Depressed people often feel worthless. Remind your friend or family member how much he or she means to you and celebrate their strengths and successes. Encourage healthy behavior and activities. Invite your loved one to join you in activities or visiting family or mutual friends. But don't push and don't expect too much too soon.

Third: Direct the person to professional help. Convincing someone who's depressed that he or she has an illness and needs professional help may take time and patience. Gently explain why you're concerned, describing changes you've seen in his or her behavior and moods. Ask if something is going on and why he or she seems down. Offer to provide referrals or to go along for an appointment. You could also phone the doctor in advance of an appointment and share your observations, which could help in the diagnosis.

Fourth: Being a close friend or family member of someone who's depressed isn't easy. Make sure you take care of yourself, especially if you find yourself becoming angry or irritable, withdrawing from activities that used to bring you joy, or worrying excessively about the situation. Take care of yourself by: 1) enlisting help from other family members and friends; 2) understanding your own feelings or needs and expressing them respectfully to the person who is depressed (i.e., "I love you, but sometimes I need some time for myself."); 3) share your feelings with a trusted friend, family member, or pastoral minister at your parish; 4) reserve time for yourself, exercise, eat a healthy diet, and do things you enjoy.

CHAPTER 11

Healings Are Not "Success Stories"

"There has got to be an end to this depression. I want to get on with my life and what I'm supposed to be." *Rad*

❧

"During my first bout with depression, I made a novena in preparation for Christmas. With as much confidence as I could muster, I asked God to heal me—that was the Christmas gift I wanted. At Midnight Mass I went to Communion anticipating this gift. As Jesus and I conversed, he very gently asked me, 'Is it okay if I don't heal you today?' This was the first time I had been aware of God's gentleness, and his gentleness in asking me moved me deeply. What could I respond but 'okay'? I have to admit, however, that I was very disappointed. Sixteen years later, I am grateful that God did not heal me that Christmas (and am amazed that I can say this). I am a stronger person today. I am a courageous person today. Perhaps my life would have been easier, but I would not have grown into who I have become. Recently I did receive my Christmas gift. I am healed." *Sr. Marie*

There is something of the absurd about depression and other mood disorders, which often bestow great gifts on their victims even as their capacity to use them is limited. Medical literature will tell you many of those suffering from depression go on to live healthy and productive lives. There are miracles and many find healing after suffering a one-time bout with depression. For others, depression recurs seasonally. And some can never completely leave depression behind, though they have returned to a seemingly "normal life." However, if all you want to achieve is a return to a life like everyone else's, you content yourself with knowing only pale reflections of joy and sorrow, meaning and love. Depression and mood disorders can be a vocation, a calling.

Sally is a forty-five-year-old woman who has suffered with chronic pain and resultant depression. She says of her experience, "Before I used to think that God could perform a miracle if he wanted to. Since he didn't, I thought I must be so awful that I wasn't worth his time. Now I see things differently. I am not cured, but Jesus has gifted me with the grace to really know that he is with me and that he loves me beyond measure. He has helped me to see that darkness and pain are not a sign of my being 'bad,' or that if I had just tried harder I would be healed by now. No, instead, Jesus is right next to me, suffering with me and whispering words of encouragement and love to me."

In the Body of Christ nothing is wasted; everything has its place, even depression.

Saint Benedict Joseph Labré

Europe was teeming with beggars on the eve of the French Revolution, and history recalls few of these faceless, nameless people. Yet, one has not been forgotten: Benedict Joseph Labré, canonized in 1883. Born in Amettes, France, on March 27, 1748, Benedict was the son of Jean Baptiste Labré and Anne Barbe Gransire. This eldest son of a farming family soon won the hearts of the neighboring villagers with his honesty, thoughtfulness, and notable intelligence. From his earliest years, Benedict was set apart for the priesthood, and he actually spent ten years studying under the tutelage of his uncles, who were also priests. Benedict desired to be ordained to the priesthood, but as time went on he did not feel attracted to the life of a parish priest. Instead, Benedict desired a stricter monastic lifestyle, a longing that grew as he read the sermons of Père Le Jeune, a fiery sixteenth-century Oratorian preacher whose harsh interpretation of Scripture and frightening depictions of judgment influenced Benedict's natural inclination to mortification. As he read and re-read Le Jeune's sermons, Benedict's salutary fear of sin grew into horror of being completely cut off from God. Eventually, painful scruples beset him and endured throughout his life.

Benedict began a life of harsh penitence in expiation for sins committed against the "good God." He also sought to join a monastery. He asked to be admitted to the Trappists, but was refused. He knocked at the door of the Carthusian monks, who also turned him down. At last, when he approached the Cistercians, he was accepted. Shortly after he experienced the joy of admittance to the novitiate of the Cistercian Abbey of Septfonts, the darkness that had been his constant companion from his youth returned.

Benedict worked hard on the grounds surrounding the monastery. When he fell gravely ill with a fever, the monks worried about this young novice who wanted so much to spend his life in penance, but who was more than strict with himself and suffered from scrupulosity and an exaggerated sense of guilt. The abbot finally had to tell Benedict that his health was not strong enough to endure the rigors of monastic life at the Abbey of Septfonts. God must have some other plan for him.

Benedict felt crushed at not being able to fulfill his life's dream. He had no desire to return home, so he resolved to find his "cloister" in the world.

In 1770, Benedict began a pilgrimage, crisscrossing Europe and praying at shrines in Germany, Italy, France, Switzerland, and Spain. He traveled about as a homeless beggar, ridiculed by many and reverenced by others who noticed the many hours he spent in prayer and in works of charity for those poorer than himself. He traveled from shrine to shrine for seven years, spending entire days in prayer at any church he came across. In truth, he lived a life more rigorous than that of a cloistered religious, exposed to all kinds of weather, suffering the hardship of the homeless. In 1777, he settled down in Rome, sleeping in the Coliseum and praying daily in the churches of the city. As he grew weaker with age and illness, he moved into shelters for the poor. On Good Friday, 1783, after the services for the Veneration of the Cross at the Sanctuary of the Madonna dei Monti, Benedict collapsed on the street and died. Benedict had told his confessor only seven days before that he was finally free of scruples, of sorrow, of every shred of his miserable sense of unworthiness. An entire life of wandering and struggle, humiliation and searching had at last opened up onto a horizon of love that left him filled with joy.

The sufferings that people embrace with God often borrow or take on some of God's immensity and mystery. People suffering from depression or other psychological illnesses are invited by God to achieve more than mere "productive living." Usefulness, productivity, appearances, and motivation are but the surface of all that life can be. Those "sidelined" by depression have the possibility of being the prophetic voices of the divine to a world completely mesmerized by efficiency and immediacy.

This is not easy. Like Benedict, you may know only the anguished struggle. You may feel useless in comparison to your former capacity for work. You may know nothing of saints and prophets whose lives were far from easy. You may even distance yourself from God. It does not matter. Christ creates a sculpture of your life, using the illnesses of body as well as sufferings of the mind to chisel the richest details. While depression may affect your dreams and lifestyle, the intensity of your spirit's yearning transforms darkness into light.

Countless health care professionals, counselors, priests, lay ministers, friends, and family members have felt blessed to witness this slow, painful, but marvelous transformation. Mildred Duff, co-founder of the Guild of Saint Benedict Joseph Labré,[1] which offers spiritual support for the emotionally troubled and the mentally ill and their family and friends, writes hundreds of letters a month to people who have shared with her their struggles and sufferings. Through these letters, Mildred glimpses the amazing work of God in the lives of those who suffer from depression. In response to one woman's anguish, Mildred wrote words that can encourage and sustain all of us on our journey.

> If words were only hugs, you would feel my loving arms around you right now. You must know and remember always that God and his Mother, who is also your mother, love you with a love that surpasses all others.
>
> You are Mary's precious child who wears the crown of thorns, and your brother Jesus is suffering with you.
>
> If these words seem too deep to understand right now, just know that Jesus knows what you are feeling now and listen to what Jesus is saying to you: "Others don't see me in you! But you must, for I am asking you: Will you wear the crown of thorns with me? Keep your heart and your head high for

together you and I will offer our suffering to save even those who reject you and me. . . ."

Yes, Benedict Joseph Labré will help you wear your "crown of thorns." Ask him for help. . . . Do the best you can under your circumstances. Just try!! That is what we ask our members to do and what I must do too. Just try!

Suggestion for prayer

My Good, my All, sole Object of my love—O come!
I long for Thee, I sigh after Thee, I wait for Thee!
Every little delay seems a thousand years! Come,
Lord Jesus, and tarry not.

Prayer of Saint Benedict Joseph Labré

For one who is depressed

Read the life of Saint Benedict Joseph Labré or Saint Thérèse of Lisieux. Think about joining the Guild of Saint Benedict.

For a friend

Thank God for the way he is working in your friend's life and for your friend's precence in your life. Share your prayer of gratitude with your friend.

Conclusion:
Eight Steps to Inner Peace

It is deeply satisfying to know that you will have in these eight steps, tools to integrate spirituality and practical guidance in order to direct your journey toward a space of greater inner expansiveness, freedom, and peace. When we are suffering from depression, our thoughts, perceptions, filters, feelings, attitudes, and expectations take an inward focus that is often highly negative in its evaluation of ourselves, others, and life. Because we ourselves are not in a hopeful and free space, our relationships often reflect our inner pain. What we most desire is to be free and to be able to freely create spaces of hope around us and with others.

I have discovered these steps over many years of searching for a more integrated method of growth. These weren't suggested by doctors or therapists or directors. They are the fruit of my journey, of the connections I have been privileged to make through the people I've met, books I've read, and experiences I've had.[1]

For over eighteen years I have struggled to get rid of the discomfort, inner sorrow, and confusion that come with depression. I have joined others as they struggled to get rid of their discomfort. I have learned that these attempts were misguided, which is why they didn't succeed. Perhaps you have had the same experience.

These steps are an invitation to enter into a process of inner spiritual and emotional direction so as to arrive at peace. They are not magic. Reading about them will not automatically create the experience they are meant to give you. I do promise you that if you take the path, walk the steps, enter the process over and over again, you will be surprised by what you receive as a result. For each person, the picture of integration brought about by these practices will look different, but for all, the result will be a life that is more at ease, thoughts that are more relaxed, relationships that are more abundant and expansive, and prayer that is more contented.

How to proceed

The steps to inner peace are a process. Each step begins by introducing a sentence that sums up the growth of that step and can be repeated during the days or weeks in which you are integrating the material into your life. The main part of the process is made up of a scriptural reflection, presentation of the content of the step, and a step-by-step practice guide. You are encouraged to work on each step for as long as you feel you are getting something out of it. When you finish the eight steps, I invite you to make them again to solidify the peace you have gained.

Step 1

I am important.

Now the LORD *said to Abram, "Go from your country and your kindred and your father's house to the land that I will show you. I will make of you a great nation, and I will bless you and make your name great, so that you will be a blessing* (Gen 12:1–2).

The Lord is always calling us forth from where we have become settled, complacent, or resigned. He promises to bless us and to make of us a blessing for others.

Rejoice in each moment exactly as it is.

Our need to manipulate an experience because we feel uncomfortable and would rather be having another more pleasant experience, is born of an inability to live in the present and to trust and rejoice in each moment *exactly as it is.* The answer is to activate awareness and appreciation of the *now,* the present moment, not regretting the past or trying to move into the future.

Practice.

Breathe. Practice breathing. Schedule your breathing practice. Take ten minutes in the morning and ten minutes in the afternoon or evening just to breathe. (Breathing through your nose is preferable—both the inhale and the exhale.) While you are breathing notice your thoughts. Are they flitting about? Are they ruminating over the past? Are they rehearsing conversations you've had with others? Are they racing into the future? Are you bored with the present and trying to get somewhere else? Are you fearful of the future? Are you projecting into the future what you think will happen, what you or someone else will probably do? Keep breathing. Start to pay attention to the sound of your breath. If necessary breathe more heavily so you can hear yourself breathing. Feel the coolness of your inhale and the warmth of your exhale. Breathing will help ground you in the present, at least for the ten minutes of your practice. Keep breathing. As you see your mind racing off, bring it gently back to your breathing. You will eventually discover that you are able to remain more in the present even outside of your practice sessions.

Abraham could hear the voice of God calling him because he was in the present moment. He wasn't making his own plans for the future. He wasn't down on himself because of something he did the day or week before. He wasn't calculating how to increase his wealth. He was simply open—rejoicing in where he was in life, ready to move wherever it seemed right to go. He was available to God's voice when it came. When God asked Abraham to get up and move, he did so. He didn't project his fears into the plan based on his experiences of the past. He simply moved where he was called, trusting that the God who was with him in the present would be with him in each present moment of the future.

You are important enough for God to speak with also. God is speaking with you. Being present to each moment and to your inner truth in each moment is the first step in hearing God's voice. God's plan for you will always be a blessing, both on you and on others.

When you feel you are comfortable in the present, are more aware of the way your mind wanders, and have established a practice of breathing, take the next step.

Step 2

I am here and now.

There the angel of the LORD *appeared to him in a flame of fire out of a bush; he looked, and the bush was blazing, yet it was not consumed. Then Moses said, "I must turn aside and look at this great sight, and see why the bush is not burned up." When the*

LORD *saw that he had turned aside to see, God called to him out of the bush, "Moses, Moses!" And he said, "Here I am." Then he said, "Come no closer! Remove the sandals from your feet, for the place on which you are standing is holy ground"* (Ex 3:2–5).

The Lord calls us nearer to him, as well as into the experiences we want to flee.

Be present to the emotional footprint of your experience.

Each event of the past, whether we consciously remember it or not, becomes present to us now as an emotion. It has what I call an emotional footprint. We may not remember the event, but the emotional footprint we feel makes it clear that we are influenced by that event: our behavior is less free, our mental belief system is affected. The emotional footprint can be labeled with a feeling word such as anxious or sad, but it also reverberates physically in our bodies as tenseness or a tightness in the stomach. Most people flee from these feelings. They flee into work, food, television, drugs, alcohol, or any other addictive behavior. These feelings, when we allow them to arise, are uncomfortable. We don't like uncomfortable feelings and flee to those that we consider more pleasurable. In doing so we miss the opportunity to become free.

Practice.

Do not flee the present. Continue your breathing practice. Each day in your practice time, draw in a small notebook a stick figure of what you feel like. Make a list of what you are experiencing. Begin with how you are feeling physically. Are your legs tight? Are your teeth clenched? Do you feel something in the pit of your stomach or is your heart racing? Listing these physical feelings will get you more in touch with how you are feeling emotionally. Continue breathing. Make a list of the emotional footprints you are experiencing right now—anger or fear or anxiety or stress or boredom. . . . Continue this practice for ten minutes so that you give yourself a chance to come toward and not flee from your experience. (If this practice creates too much emotional anxiety, you may wish to do it with a person you trust, perhaps a therapist or a counselor.) You will discover shifts beginning to happen in the energy connected with these emotions. Over time the energy will begin to dissipate. Stay with this practice consistently, welcoming whatever emotional footprints surface without labeling them good or bad. The uncomfortable feelings, held without condition, have the most power to leave us changed and more at peace.

Moses saw the burning bush and decided to check it out. He was aware of what was happening around him and sensitive to his feelings of curiosity. Moses went toward the experience. As the Lord revealed to Moses his mission to return to Egypt and free God's people from slavery, Moses experienced feelings of unworthiness, anxiety, and resistance, and he tried to get the Lord to send someone else. Finally, the Lord became angry with Moses's objections to his mission, gave Moses a spokesperson in his brother Aaron, and said, "Go!" Moses was aware of his feelings. He could have gotten up and fled the Lord's presence, but instead he kept bringing his feelings up to the Lord. He was present to the emotional footprints of this event as they passed through his heart and mind. And, remaining in the present moment, he worked out the plan for the mission on which he was being sent.

Every day you encounter "burning bushes" that give rise to feelings within you. These events, conversations, and people may seem to be problems, hassles, or obstacles, but in reality they are the way in which God is helping you grow and integrate the emotional footprints that still haunt you and block feelings of well-being.

When you see that you are more adept at noticing and listing your feelings and the physical sensations they create, you may move on to Step 3.

Step 3

This moment is valuable.

In the sixth month the angel Gabriel was sent by God to a town in Galilee called Nazareth, to a virgin engaged to a man whose name was Joseph, of the house of David. The virgin's name was Mary. And he came to her and said, "Greetings, favored one! The Lord is with you. . . . And now, you will conceive in your womb and bear a son, and you will name him Jesus" (Lk 1:26–31, 38).

Sometimes wonderful things happen in our lives, such as, for Mary, the Annunciation. Most of the time, however, our days are a succession of not-so-interesting events and a whole lot of waiting.

Value what is happening in your life right now.

We have an insatiable mental hunger for something other than what we are experiencing or doing right now. We buy one item and we instantly want the next upgraded version. We achieve one goal and are dissatisfied because we look to the next. We are in one situation and automatically "drop it," just like children discard their toys, in favor of the next stimulating experience. We dread the drudgery and boredom of the journey in favor of the perceived excitement of the destination, only to find the destination less appealing than something else. *This* moment is important. *This* moment is enough. *This* moment is perfect just as it is.

Practice.

This moment is valuable. Continue your breathing practice. Now add some words to your breaths. *This* (on the inhale) *moment* (on the exhale) *just as* (on the inhale) *it is* (on the exhale) *is* (on the inhale) *perfect* (on the exhale). When you find yourself bored during the day, recall this phrase and practice breathing for a few moments using these words. On the road, while cooking or changing diapers, waiting for a meeting to begin (or finish!), trying to fall asleep, waiting for someone to arrive—learn to value each moment. Become consciously aware of your feelings but in a more nuanced way. With this list of words commonly used to express feelings, try to understand better your internal experiences:

- ○ Gloomy
- ○ Dejected
- ○ Apprehensive
- ○ Upset
- ○ Agony
- ○ Disappointed
- ○ Appalled
- ○ Frantic
- ○ Apathetic
- ○ Arrogant
- ○ Cold
- ○ Perturbed
- ○ Resistant
- ○ Shy
- ○ Skeptical
- ○ Weary
- ○ Exasperated
- ○ Enraged
- ○ Angry
- ○ Cranky
- ○ Edgy
- ○ Cautious

- ○ Fearful
- ○ Worried
- ○ Hungry
- ○ Amused
- ○ Ecstatic
- ○ Joyful
- ○ Jubilant
- ○ Radiant
- ○ Tickled
- ○ Expectant
- ○ Loving
- ○ Proud
- ○ Surprised
- ○ Intense
- ○ Pleased
- ○ Refreshed
- ○ Thankful

- ○ Relaxed
- ○ Relieved
- ○ Free
- ○ Confident
- ○ Contented
- ○ Carefree
- ○ Composed
- ○ Excited
- ○ Alert
- ○ Animated
- ○ Curious
- ○ Focused
- ○ Hopeful
- ○ Inspired
- ○ Invigorated
- ○ Spellbound

After the angel appeared to Mary and announced that she was to be the Mother of God, her next recorded activities are interesting. She didn't go out and tell her mother, "Mom, guess what just happened. What should I do? Oh my goodness, we should tell the family! We need to get ready! God is coming!" Instead, she did what the angel had indicated to her. Her cousin Elizabeth was with child. She was elderly. She was alone. Mary took a long journey to see Elizabeth and help her with the birth of her child and the first weeks of his care. She didn't seem concerned about what her family knew or thought, or even what Joseph was going to think. She didn't seem worried about the fact that she was obviously with child and nobody knew how. She seemed to enjoy and love what was happening moment by moment through the difficulty of the journey to her cousin, the time she spent with mute Zechariah, the journey back, the confusion and pain in Joseph who wanted to divorce her quietly. . . . It takes a great strength to live in the present. However, she must have been interiorly aware of how she felt. Perhaps she spoke quietly about her worries and plans with Elizabeth.

During the day you have these "annunciation" moments also. It may be something you read, a stray comment on the radio or from a friend, a surging feeling of joy listening to music, the feeling of reverence that comes over you in a church or watching a sunset. This may take about twenty-five minutes of your day. The other twenty-three hours and thirty-five minutes just have to be "gotten through" until the next great annunciation, unless these other moments and hours of the day become unexplored treasures. For they are indeed treasures! Within them are buried the feelings that, if acknowledged, could make you much more alive.

Continue your breathing and recite the phrase for this step as often as possible, until you treasure the beauty of the uneventful moments of your day. Then move on to the next step.

Step 4

Everything is okay just as it is.

And that is what the soldiers did. Meanwhile, standing near the cross of Jesus were his mother, and his mother's sister, Mary the wife of Clopas, and Mary Magdalene (Jn 19:25).

Sad, crucifying situations often cause us to spiral into depression. "Everything is going wrong. There is no future for me." However, the women stood beneath the cross. They stayed with Jesus to the end.

Reality is reliable.

It is only human to have ideals, plans, expectations. And it is only human to feel disillusioned when those ideals aren't realized, plans are canceled, and expectations aren't lived up to by us or by the people around us. By becoming aware of how we have frozen other people or a situation into expectations, and by softening the demands we make on others or ourselves, we free ourselves up to rejoice in reality as it is. Reality is where, moment by moment, we discover who God is, who others are, and who we are.

Practice.

Everything is okay just as it is. Continue your breathing practice. Continue to add the same words to your breaths. *This* (on the inhale) *moment* (on the exhale) *just as* (on the inhale) *it is* (on the exhale) *is* (on the inhale) *perfect* (on the exhale). We have learned to be conscious of our feelings, which are red flags alerting us to the fact that our needs are or are not being met. Our life is enriched when our basic needs are met. Situations and events, conversations and just casually heard comments can trigger feelings and raise up needs we have. The other persons involved in the triggering situations may or may not be able to meet our needs.

Here we are talking about the universal life-enriching needs we all share. We employ different strategies and methods for meeting these needs and we can differ with others about the advisability or benefit of one or another strategy. However, we can all agree on these common human needs:

○ Peace of mind
○ Trust
○ Presence
○ Inspiration
○ Beauty
○ Harmony
○ Nurturing
○ Competency
○ Intimacy
○ Creativity
○ Freedom
○ Autonomy
○ Connection
○ Clarity

○ Cooperation
○ Community
○ Support
○ Safety
○ Play
○ Celebration
○ Gratitude
○ Healing
○ Contribution (to be seen)
○ Attention (to be heard)
○ Acknowledgement (to be known)

During your breathing practice, take a notebook and divide a page in half. On the left side of the page write the word "feelings." On the right side write the word "needs." Think of a situation, event, or conversation that made you feel especially excited or uncomfortable. Explore the feelings that you experience as you reflect on the situation, the emotional footprint, any physical sensations, as well as the needs you have which are, or are not, being met. Be patient with yourself. This is like learning a new language: *your* language. As you learn to self-connect, you will find yourself feeling more and more at ease. Do this twice a day.

Exploring the needs that Jesus and the women had as they stood beneath the cross is a contemplative exercise that is practical both for increasing our self-connection and our connection with God. Jesus, as he hung on the cross, may have felt sad, distressed, lonely, afraid, full of pain, weary, and agitated. He also may have been, at a very deep level, peaceful, radiant, and hopeful. He may have felt the following needs arising as he died on the cross: a need for understanding and safety, a need for purpose as he saw that all his apostles save one had fled, a need for love, a need for justice, and a need for consideration. The women also had their feelings and needs as they stood there, probably ridiculed by the crowd, unable to comprehend what was ultimately happening as they watched their Master die. They had needs for understanding and compassion and support. They needed safety and assurance. They desired clarity about what was happening. They wanted to be healed. Jesus couldn't get his needs met by the crowd and neither could the women who stayed with him. They had to reach deep within themselves and rely on the mutual support and understanding of their tiny, tight-knit group as they stood on Mount Calvary. They also had to process their disillusionment. It was not all supposed to end now. Especially not in this way. Disillusionment leads to feelings of sadness and depression.

Awareness of our needs is crucial to having them met. We may have the same needs that Jesus and the women had on Calvary, or we may have others. As we list them, patterns may emerge. We may also discover that simply knowing what these needs are can help us stop demanding that they be met by others, or by life itself. Instead we can learn to hold them gently and with a bit of curiosity. Over time we will discover strategies for meeting them, either through self-nurturance or through friendships with safe people. Actually, each of us is responsible for getting our own basic needs met. The experience of the cross and the resurrection assures us that we will discover in reality treasures we didn't realize existed.

Spend time daily getting in touch with your universal needs, understanding how they are, or are not, being met. When this practice has become a habit, move on to Step 5.

Step 5

The providence of God looks out for my good.

Now the birth of Jesus the Messiah took place in this way. When his mother Mary had been engaged to Joseph, but before they lived together, she was found to be with child from the Holy Spirit. Her husband Joseph, being a righteous man and unwilling to expose her to public disgrace, planned to dismiss her quietly. But just when he had resolved to do this, an angel of the Lord appeared to him in a dream and said, "Joseph, son of David, do not be afraid to take Mary as your wife, for the child conceived in her is from the Holy Spirit" (Mt 1:18–20).

Joseph sized up the situation and decided what would be the most just move: to put Mary away quietly. God had other plans. God usually does. And they're always better than ours.

Put your trust in God's providential care for you.

We have been getting in touch with our thoughts, our feelings, our needs. In the end, however, after we allow the emotional footprint of an event to resonate within our awareness, having patiently watched it during our breathing practice, we need to make a decision on how to move forward. Here are three keys: 1) Often, we find our choices are rooted in blame. Observe what you are thinking about the person or situation as you begin to make a choice. If you do not perceive that this situation or person is a gift of God, you are not ready to make a choice about what to do. Why? Because you are closed to inspiration and grace. You are unconsciously acting out of anger or revenge. Unfortunately, this way of acting is all too human and must be unlearned if you wish to be at peace. Try instead to develop a certain empathy toward your needs and find life-giving ways to meet them. 2) If you are making a decision about the person or situation based on what you want the other person to do, stop! You will be more effective if your first desire is to connect with the other person who also has his or her own feelings and needs. Before making a decision, you might ask how they are feeling about the situation and what they need right now. 3) If possible, after making a decision, wait twenty-four hours before implementing it. Ask God for his light. He may have a better idea.

Practice.

Choices about how to handle people and situations happen daily. Each evening look back on one situation, and in your notebook write about the following:

1. How do I feel about the person or situation?
2. What do I need in this situation?
3. If there were no constraints on me, what would I want to do? (Here you can see the strength of your deepest instincts held in check by the need or desire to be nice or good.)
4. According to what I've learned from parents or society, what do I think I'm supposed to do? (This answer often reveals a direction too narrow for the complexities of a situation. Often it is a twisted version of a good principle. For example: Christians aren't supposed to get angry so I should just take her verbal abuse and smile. In answering questions three and four, as you identify thoughts and desires that have a powerful controlling effect on you

even if unconsciously, your heart will experience more spaciousness and gentleness.)

5. What do I think the other person is feeling?

6. What might the other person need?

7. Ask Jesus what he would like to say to the other person? What does he want for the other person?

8. Look back at your needs, those of the others, and the words Jesus may have said to the other person. What request could you make that would encompass the needs of both of you? Maybe the request would be just for yourself, or just for the other person. The request should be something small that can easily be accomplished.

Joseph must have thought long and hard when Mary returned pregnant after her visit to Elizabeth. Probably he was devastated and possibily angry. If he had made a decision based on those feelings, he would have dragged Mary into the village square for the prescribed punishment of stoning. However, the Scriptures say that he was unwilling to expose her to the law, but sought to divorce her quietly; he then went to sleep on his decision. He took into account both his feelings and needs and hers. He reached deep into his inner resources and came up with a plan that would free him of the engagement while protecting her from public outrage. An angel, however, revealed to him that God was working in Mary and that he was to take her as his wife and name the child Jesus. Because Joseph was sufficiently free of his original feelings, he was open to the plan of God and was prompt to switch directions even at great cost to himself and his reputation.

Following the eight-part process listed above, will open you to the possibility of hearing God's voice because you will be free from the necessity of seeking revenge and exacting justice. You will not only find greater peace, you will create around your-self spaces of peace which others will find attractive.

Stay with this step until you have made this practice a daily habit. Don't forget to continue your breathing practice to remain in the present moment.

Step 6

I am strong when I am weak.

Therefore, to keep me from being too elated, a thorn was given me in the flesh, a messenger of Satan to torment me, to keep me from being too elated. Three times I appealed to the Lord about this, that it would leave me, but he said to me, "My grace is sufficient for you, for power is made perfect in weak-ness." So, I will boast all the more gladly of my weaknesses, so that the power of Christ may dwell in me. Therefore I am con-tent with weaknesses, insults, hardships, persecutions, and calamities for the sake of Christ; for whenever I am weak, then I am strong (2 Cor 12:7b–10).

Saint Paul was able to hear something different than what he wanted to hear because he was in conversation and relation-ship with the Other.

Believe that your struggle with depression has meaning.

When you are depressed, many things lose their attraction. One of them is prayer. Relationships become difficult, and your relationship with God will also hit rocky waters. You feel like withdrawing from others. You will want to react the same way with God. Nevertheless, you are always in relation with God because, whether you believe it or not, you are created out of love. You certainly didn't create yourself. Neither do you keep yourself in existence. You are loved into being minute by minute. So if your relationship with God is rocky, act as you do in any rocky relationship. Cry out. Get angry. Demand answers. Request a change. The most moving passages of Scripture are the human cry of pain and incomprehension. Even Jesus asked that the divine plan be changed on the night before his death-walk to Calvary. Look at Jeremiah, Isaiah, Moses, Paul, Peter. . . God is not frightened by your reality.

Practice.

I am strong when I am weak. Continue your breathing practice but add these words: *I* (on the inhale) *am* (on the exhale) *with* (on the inhale) *you* (on the exhale) *here* (on the inhale) *and now* (on the exhale). Pay attention to the emotional footprint that accompanies this prayer. What are you feeling? What are the sensations in your body? Don't be afraid if you feel resentment, anger, disgust, revenge, or bitterness. Talk to God out of the energy that accompanies these feelings and continue the breathing practice, giving your emotional reactions an opportunity to shift and dissipate. Then tell God what you need, using the list of universal needs in Step 4.

The three-fold request of Paul that he be freed from the "thorn in the flesh" mirrors Jesus's three-fold request to his Father in the Garden of Gethsemane that he be freed from the cup he was being given to drink. Both spoke openly to God about what they were feeling and thought they needed. They were suggesting a better way. However, God knows we have needs that we haven't discovered yet or which are just too scary to own at the moment. For example, I have often wanted to be released from an assignment because I felt the need for security, stability, or simply more space. However, in every case, I have eventually come to love the new work I was asked to do and have developed my skills and personality in ways that would never have been possible if I had not agreed to do what had been asked. God knows I have a strong need for meaning, purpose, a sense of integrity, and the feeling that I am contributing. He often says no to my requests because he knows that if he relented I would never satisfy these profoundly existential needs for authenticity and self-expression. It is difficult to reach deep inside and come up with the inner resources needed to go on and to grow in new ways, but the effort is profoundly satisfying. I think Jesus and Paul had similar experiences. God knew the depths of their hearts and their capacity for loving and caring, and he gave them what they really wanted.

This reflection offers another way to look at needs and possibly a fresh way of understanding how you and God can relate, and how you can converse regarding issues that touch upon your depression. This would be helpful to share with a soul mate, spiritual director, or therapist.

This step asks for a profound change of mentality and desire on your part. This might be a good place for you to take a breather. Go back over the first six steps. Be gentle with yourself as your soul gradually finds the trust and courage to open up to God's plans for your life.

Step 7

I am a gift to others, just as I am today.

[Paul] lived there two whole years at his own expense and welcomed all who came to him, proclaiming the kingdom of God and teaching about the Lord Jesus Christ with all boldness and without hindrance (Acts 28:30–31).

A triumphant ending to the account of the life of the Apostle Paul: the man who had been chased out of towns and villages for his preaching, caused trouble with the elders in Jerusalem, cried with sorrow and bitterness over the problems in some of the communities he had founded, upset the status quo with new ideas, which he said were a commission from the Lord Jesus, and lived with mistreatment, mistrust, misunderstanding, loneliness, hunger, suffering, and sorrow since the day Jesus had appeared to him on the road to Damascus. And here he is again, preaching with full assurance and joy.

See your life from the long view.
You are a gift to the world, just as you are.

The struggles and upsets and disappointments and aggravations of life tend to narrow our vision and distort our perspective. Instead of seeing who we have been created to be, we see who we feel like right now. Gifts, joy-filled experiences, happy memories of the past dissipate. Plans and dreams crumple. We are in the now, but a now that is dominated by ugly feelings, not truth.

Practice.

I am a gift to others, just as I am today. Renew your breathing practice using the words: *I am with you here and now* as learned in Step 6. By now you should be spontaneously carrying out this practice during the day when you have a break from mental occupations. In your notebook take a small survey of your life. Without getting tangled up in stories and memories, simply list the events and situations that are part of your life this year. Go back nine or ten years, identify the year, and try to remember what was happening during that time of your life.

Go back ten more years, identify the year, and try to remember what was happening during that period of your life. And so on, until you reach your birth. In the earliest years of your life you won't be able to remember actual events most likely, but pay attention to the energy you feel as you think about that time in your life. This is how your body remembers what happened. For the next couple of weeks, when you pray or during your breathing practice, take the list you have made, read it through. Choose one event and follow the eight-part process outlined in Step 5. One by one, integrate these memories into your history by making peace with them. Allow the energy associated with them, which has built up in your spirit and in your body, to shift and dissipate. When you have finished this process do the following: 1) imagine these situations one by one and see them radiating light and hope; wish well-being, grace, and joy to anyone involved in the memory; 2) list all the things in your life for which you are grateful; 3) write a prayer or complete a ritual of thanksgiving.

Think of Paul's life, which was not easy. It was chaotic; relationships were tempestuous; his personality was fiery, especially at the start of his discipleship; he made mistakes, became frustrated and discouraged; the apostles Peter and James, particularly James, were not pleased with him and didn't understand what he was doing; the Church in Jerusalem sent spies after him intent on counteracting his teaching. They sowed unrest and confusion in the communities he had founded. You get the point. His life was like ours. And yet he made peace with it, just as it was. In the end, as we grow older, we all must do this. We must make peace with our life just as it has been and realize that we *are* God's gift to the universe, just as we are. We don't need to be rich, beautiful, successful, important, perfect, or accomplished to be an instrument in God's hands. We only have to be *in God's hands.* If we leave those hands, fall out of them for any reason, we only have to jump right back into them, for God is always waiting for our desire to be with him and in him once more.

As you reflect upon your life you may find yourself feeling depressed or sorrowful over past events. Probably Paul also regretted some things about his life. Paul, however, never lost sight of his calling and mission. Whenever Paul was called before the authorities to give an account of his activity, he always recounted the event on the road to Damascus when Jesus appeared to Paul, called Paul, and told Paul to bring his name to the nations. We may not have had a personal visit from Jesus, but we have received our Christian identity through Baptism and perhaps also Confirmation. We can bear him in our hearts and in our lives through the Eucharist. We are, in the end, whom God made us to be: his own. That is the most important part of your history. You can rely on God's fidelity, just as Paul did.

This step will take quite a bit of time to complete. It is possible to take just one period of your life at a time. At another point, or when doing the process again, you can integrate another period of your life.

Step Eight

I am with God in this.

In those days a decree went out from Emperor Augustus that all the world should be registered. Joseph also went from the town of Nazareth in Galilee to Judea, to the city of David called Bethlehem, because he was descended from the house and family of David. He went to be registered with Mary, to whom he was engaged and who was expecting a child. While they were there, the time came for her to deliver her child. And she gave birth to her firstborn son and wrapped him in bands of cloth, and laid him in a manger, because there was no place for them in the inn (Lk 2:1, 4–7).

God wanted to be "with us" and so he sent Jesus, born like us, in fact, like us in *all* things except sin.

God is with you.

You have learned many things during this eight-week practice. You have learned to welcome the uncomfortableness of your emotional footprints without fleeing from them. You have discovered that mental habits and entrenched perspectives have begun to soften and become more ordered to reality. You probably will have found yourself really listening to others with care and compassion and walking more quickly on your spiritual journey with God. Perhaps you have found that you are now more compassionate with yourself and more patient with others. All of these treasures are gifts of presence. Presence to yourself, to others, and to God. Presence and connection.

Practice.

I am with God in this. Renew your breathing practice, but let your breathing now support self-awareness and your presence to God by adding these words: *I* (on the inhale) *am* (on the exhale) *with* (on the inhale) *you* (on the exhale), *in* (on the inhale) *you* (on the exhale), *through* (on the inhale) *you* (on the exhale). *You* (on the inhale) *are* (on the exhale) *with* (on the inhale) *me* (on the exhale), *in* (on the inhale) *me* (on the exhale), *through* (on the inhale) *me* (on the exhale).

Through the entire journey of the Chosen People as narrated in the Hebrew Scriptures and by the birth of Jesus as

Emmanuel, it is clear that God's desire is to be here with us, walking through our lives, living through us. He wanted to experience our life from the inside out so that we could experience the life of God from the inside out. Through the Holy Spirit, God becomes the new life principle within us. By deepening our life in the Spirit, we finally find liberation, joy, and peace.

This is the end of the steps to finding inner peace. Enjoy the new sense of ease and confidence that you have found. Continue to practice daily the tools you have found most helpful. And make the journey again when you are ready. Each time you will go deeper in your self-connectedness, your capacity for intimacy with others, and your freedom to be open to the divine.

Epilogue

Do you find yourself in the dark night of depression, this place of hopeless, stripping loneliness and meaninglessness? All hope and faith may seem truly extinguished. Saint John of the Cross, who was imprisoned in complete darkness for nine months because of his beliefs, profoundly experienced this desolation and depression. He described the experience as the soul feeling itself to be impure and miserable, unworthy of God or any other creature. In mental suffering and depression, it may be nearly impossible for you to know how much of what you experience is mental illness and how much is the baffling experience of the dark night through which God leads those whom he loves. Fortunately, you do not need to sort that out.

Thankfully, depression is no more a period of complete loss than is the winter season. The place where you are can open up and become new life. It is a creative time, even if you do not perceive it as such. The saints you have met in this book and the key moments in the history of salvation that have been presented in its pages have shown that vital actions can be accomplished even in weakness. God does not need our strength; God prefers to work with weakness. God himself became weak. In our humbled spirit, God's creative Spirit is freer to work in us. Spiritual author Maria Boulding[1] once said that we often allow God's radiance to shine more purely through our lives in times of winter darkness than in our summer prosperity.

God seems to prefer this pattern. From Abraham, who walked into an uncertain future on the word of a God he did not know, to Jesus, crucified in weakness and failure, it becomes clear that God works in no other way.

Through weakness, something new breaks into our world. Through you, something new is born for the rest of us who hurry briskly by. You have a vocation that the world needs. In your suffering, you become a great prophet by bearing Christ's cross with his strength and in his light.

Immersed in the ever Creative Power
that penetrates my private world
in rhythms sure and confident,
I open to the mysterious Presence
that silently weaves people and events,
forever overlapping lives and times,
giving rise to indelible impression
upon the spatial memory
and we, travelers of current history,
evoke in one another
a need for response and belonging
in the world we call our lives.
No one without another,
no man without his past,
vital exchange of intimacies
impress a heart forever.

Today is the unfolding mystery
that bespeaks eternal motion,
whose purpose, beyond the stars,
defies finite contingency.

Sr. Thomas Halpin, FSP
June 8, 1994

Notes

Introduction

1. Survey conducted by the Centers for Disease Control and Prevention, reported in the *Morbidity and Mortality Weekly Report* (MMWR) 59, no. 38 (October 1, 2010): 1229–1235. See also erratum issued for this report.

2. M.E.P. Seligman, *Learned Optimism* (1990). Quoted on the website: www.clinical-depression.co.uk/dlp/depression-information/major-depression-facts/.

3. Ibid.

4. Names and details have been changed to respect their privacy.

Chapter 1

1. Prosper Goepfert, *The Life of the Venerable Francis Mary Paul Libermann: Founder of the Congregation of the Holy Heart of Mary* (Dublin: M. H. Gil and Son, 1880), 103.

2. www.spiritans.com/libermannpage.htm.

Chapter 2

1. Cf. www.medicinenet.com/script/main/art.asp?articlekey=24251.

2. Cf. www.webmd.com/balance/features/america-psyche-post-911.

3. J. Hamblem, M. Friedman, P. Schnurr, *Anniversary Reactions: Research Findings* (National Center for Post Traumatic Stress Disorder, 2010).

4. Jane Frances de Chantal, *A Simple Life: Wisdom from Jane Frances de Chantal* (Boston: Pauline Books and Media, 2011).

5. Francis de Sales, *Courage in Chaos: Wisdom from Francis de Sales* (Boston: Pauline Books and Media, 2011).

6. Ibid.

Chapter 5

1. For more information on compassionate, nonviolent communication, an internationally tried model of communication developed by Marshall Rosenberg, PhD, that increases understanding, cooperation, and the resolution of conflict between diverse groups and people, the following may be helpful: Jane Marantz Connor, PhD, and Dian Killian, PhD, *Connecting Across Differences: A Guide to Compassionate, Nonviolent Communication* (Hungry Duck Press, 2005).

Chapter 7

1. Gino Concetti, "Edith Stein," *L'Osservatore Romano* (April 27, 1987): 3–4.

2. Ibid.

Chapter 11

1. If you would like more information on the Guild of Saint Benedict Joseph Labré, send a letter or request to P.O. Box 200, Buzzards Bay, MA 02532.

Conclusion

1. Some of these connections include: *The Cloud of Unknowing: And The Book of Privy Counseling* by William Johnston (New York: Image, 1996); *Into the Silent Land: A Guide to the Christian Practice of Contemplation* by Martin Laird (New York: Oxford University Press, 2006); *The Practice of the Presence of God* by Brother Lawrence of the Resurrection (New York, Destiny Image, 2007); *Abandonment to Divine Providence*, by Jean Pierre de Caussade (New York: Image, 1993); the movement of mindfulness begun by Jon Kabat-Zin (whose presentations can be found on youtube.com); a friend who taught me how to live in the present moment; the writings of Thomas Keating, particularly: *Daily Reader for Contemplative Living: Excerpts from the Works of Father Thomas Keating, OCSO, Sacred Scripture, and Other Spiritual Writings* by authors Thomas Keating and Stephanie S. Iachetta (New York: Continuum, 2009);

Three Keys to Self-Understanding: An Innovative and Effective Combination of the Myers-Briggs Type Indicator Assessment Tool, the Enneagram, and Inner-Child Healing, by Pat Wyman (Gainesville: Center for Applications of Psychological Type, 2002).

Epilogue

1. Cf. Maria Boulding, *The Coming of God* (Collegeville: Liturgical Press, 1986), 41.